Mastering

GMRS Radio

From

Beginner To Pro

The Definitive Guide to Features, Setup, Programming, Communication Techniques, Troubleshooting, Tips, Tricks, and Hidden Hacks for Power Users

Kai J. Tempest

Mastering Unreal Engine 5 from Beginner to Pro: The Definitive Guide to Building High-Quality Games, Immersive Virtual Worlds, and Advanced Interactive Contents.

First edition. April 2025.

Copyright © 2025 Kai J. Tempest

Written by Kai J. Tempest

TABLE OF CONTENTS

TABLE OF CONTENTS II

CHAPTER 1 1

INTRODUCTION TO GMRS RADIOS 1

    WHAT IS GMRS? 1
    WHY CHOOSE GMRS RADIO? 1
    WHO SHOULD USE GMRS RADIOS? 4

CHAPTER 2 7

GETTING STARTED WITH GMRS RADIOS 7

    UNDERSTANDING GMRS RADIO FREQUENCIES 7
    GMRS FREQUENCY BANDS 7
    UNDERSTANDING CHANNEL NUMBERS 8
    GMRS REPEATER CHANNELS 8
    POWER AND FREQUENCY 8
    THE ROLE OF THE FCC IN GMRS FREQUENCIES 9
    FREQUENCY AND ANTENNA CONSIDERATIONS 9
    WHY FREQUENCY MATTERS 9
    INTERFERENCE AND CONGESTION OF GMRS FREQUENCIES 10

TYPES OF GMRS RADIOS AVAILABLE 10

REQUIRED LICENSES AND REGULATIONS 16

    WHO NEEDS A GMRS LICENSE? 16
    HOW TO OBTAIN A GMRS LICENSE 17
    GMRS REGULATIONS AND USAGE RULES 21
    PENALTIES FOR VIOLATING GMRS REGULATIONS 23

CHAPTER 3 24

SETTING UP YOUR GMRS RADIO 24

    GMRS RADIO INSTALLATION 24

SETTING UP A GMRS REPEATER 35

    REQUIREMENTS FOR SETTING UP A GMRS REPEATER 35
    HOW TO SET UP A GMRS REPEATER 36
    HOW DOES A GMRS REPEATER WORK? 37
    HOW TO CONNECT TO GMRS REPEATER 37
    USE A GMRS REPEATER FOR LONGER RANGE 38
        What Do You Need to Use a GMRS Repeater? 38
        How Do You Use a GMRS Repeater for Longer Range? 39
    HOW DO REPEATERS WORK 39

HOW TO FIND AND ASK FOR PERMISSION TO USE GMRS REPEATERS 40
WHAT ARE THE GMRS REPEATER TONES? 40
Open Repeaters and the 141.3 Hz GMRS Travel Tone 41

POWER SOURCE AND BATTERY MANAGEMENT 41

GPS INTEGRATION AND LOCATION SERVICES 43

PRIVACY AND SECURITY CONSIDERATIONS 45

EASY WAY TO TUNE A GMRS ANTENNA 47

GMRS ANTENNA BASICS: WHAT IS SWR? 48

EASIEST WAY TO SET GMRS RADIO SWR 49

GMRS RADIO LINEAR AMPLIFIER 52
CAN YOU USE A LINEAR AMPLIFIER FOR GMRS RADIO? 52

HOW TO LEGALLY BOOST GMRS RADIO POWER 53
SETTING THE GMRS RADIO SWR 53

PROPER ANTENNA PLACEMENT FOR GMRS RADIO ANTENNAS 53

REPLACING YOUR STOCK MOBILE OR HANDHELD GMRS ANTENNA WITH A HIGH GAIN
MODEL 54

OTHER WAYS TO INCREASE GMRS RADIO RANGE 55
TWO EXAMPLES OF GMRS RADIO RANGE 56

CHAPTER 4 58

OPERATING YOUR GMRS RADIO 58

OVERVIEW OF KEY FEATURES AND BUTTONS 58

MAIN CONTROLS AND PARTS OF THE RADIO 59
LCD DISPLAY 59

HOW TO MAKE AND RECEIVE CALLS 61

HOW TO RECEIVE A CALL 61

CHANNELS, PRIVACY CODES, AND THEIR USES 62
CHANNELS 62
PRIVACY CODES 63
HOW CHANNELS AND PRIVACY CODES WORK TOGETHER 64
PRACTICAL APPLICATIONS OF CHANNELS AND PRIVACY CODES 64

COMMUNICATION BEST PRACTICES 65

GMRS RADIO ETIQUETTE 69

CHAPTER 5 .... **73**

GMRS RADIO SETTINGS AND CONFIGURATION **73**

ADJUSTING SQUELCH AND VOLUME LEVELS 73
SQUELCH SWITCH 74

CHANNEL SCANNING CONFIGURATION **75**

RADIO SYSTEM INTEGRATION AND INTERFACING **77**

SCENARIO: LOGISTICS COMPANY INTEGRATION OF GMRS 78

CHAPTER 6 .... **81**

GMRS RADIO PROGRAMMING **81**

INTRODUCTION TO GMRS RADIO PROGRAMMING 81
BASIC RADIO PROGRAMMING TOOLS 81

STEP-BY-STEP GUIDE TO PROGRAMMING GMRS RADIOS **83**

PROGRAMMING FREQUENCIES IN THE RADIO **85**

TROUBLESHOOTING COMMON PROGRAMMING ISSUES 87

CHAPTER 7 .... **92**

ADVANCED GMRS FEATURES AND FUNCTIONS **92**

GPS INTEGRATION 92

WEATHER ALERTS AND NOAA CHANNELS **93**

NOAA WEATHER FREQUENCIES 94

ENCRYPTION AND PRIVACY **95**

GET TO KNOW GMRS ENCRYPTION: WHAT YOU NEED TO KNOW 96
DECIPHERING THE SECRETS OF GMRS ENCRYPTION 97
BECOMING A GMRS ENCRYPTION PRO 97
DEVELOP ADVANCED SKILLS 98
UNLOCKING THE BENEFITS OF GMRS ENCRYPTION 98
ENCRYPTING VOICE SIGNALS 99
    Simple Inversion Encryption *99*
    Hopping Inversion Encryption *100*
    Rolling Code Inversion Encryption *100*
    DES and AES Encryption *101*
MANAGING ENCRYPTION KEYS IN A COMPLEX ENVIRONMENT 102
COMPATIBILITY OF ENCRYPTION BETWEEN DIFFERENT BRANDS 103

CHAPTER 8 .... **104**

INTEGRATION WITH OTHER RADIO SYSTEMS **104**

COMPATIBILITY WITH FRS RADIOS 104
FRS...104
GMRS..105
UTILIZING FRS AND GMRS RADIOS FOR LOCAL DISASTER COMMUNICATION...........107

CONNECT TO GMRS REPEATERS AROUND YOU **110**
HOW TO FIND OPEN GMRS REPEATERS AROUND ME...110
HOW TO CONNECT A GMRS RADIO TO GMRS REPEATERS AROUND YOU.................111
CROSS-BAND OPERATIONS AND INTEROPERABILITY 113

CHAPTER 9 .... **115**

TROUBLESHOOTING AND MAINTENANCE **115**
COMMON GMRS RADIO ISSUES AND SOLUTIONS..115

MAINTAINING YOUR GMRS RADIO FOR LONGEVITY **119**
HOW TO MAXIMIZE BATTERY LIFE 121

CHAPTER 10 .... **124**

GMRS RADIO ACCESSORIES... **124**
ESSENTIAL ACCESSORIES FOR GMRS RADIOS...124

HOW TO CHOOSE THE RIGHT ANTENNA **128**
UPGRADING YOUR GMRS RADIO FOR BETTER PERFORMANCE 132

CHAPTER 11 .... **136**

UNDERSTANDING GMRS REGULATIONS AND LAWS **136**
LEGAL USAGE OF GMRS RADIOS 136
TIPS FOR STAYING COMPLIANT WITH GMRS REGULATIONS 140

CHAPTER 12 .... **145**

GMRS RADIO IN DIFFERENT ENVIRONMENTS **145**
USING GMRS RADIOS FOR OUTDOOR ADVENTURES...145
UNDERSTANDING THE BENEFITS OF GMRS RADIOS FOR OUTDOOR ADVENTURES 145
HOW TO PICK THE BEST GMRS RADIO FOR OUTDOOR USE....................................146
SETTING UP GMRS RADIOS FOR OUTDOOR COMMUNICATION 146
USING GMRS RADIOS IN REMOTE AREAS...147
SAFETY AND EMERGENCY USE OF GMRS RADIOS...148
MAINTAINING GMRS RADIOS DURING YOUR ADVENTURE.....................................148

GMRS RADIOS IN EMERGENCY SITUATIONS **149**
WHY GMRS RADIOS ARE IMPORTANT IN EMERGENCIES 149
SETTING UP FOR EMERGENCY USE..149

USING GMRS RADIOS FOR COMMUNICATION DURING A CRISIS...150
STAYING INFORMED WITH GMRS RADIOS..151
SAFETY AND EMERGENCY PROTOCOLS FOR GMRS USE 152
THE ROLE OF GMRS RADIOS IN LONG-TERM EMERGENCIES 152
BEST PRACTICES FOR USING GMRS IN URBAN AREAS 153

CONCLUSION **158**

CHAPTER 1

INTRODUCTION TO GMRS RADIOS

What is GMRS?

GMRS stands for General Mobile Radio Service. It is a sort of two-way radio communication that uses frequencies between 462 MHz and 467 MHz. People regularly use GMRS radios for outdoor activities such as hiking, camping, and off-roading, as well as for emergency communications.

Even though they share certain frequencies, GMRS and FRS (Family Radio Service) radios are not the same thing. The key distinction is that GMRS radios can transmit at significantly greater power levels, up to 50 watts, whereas FRS radios are limited to just 2 watts. This increased power implies that GMRS radios have a greater range and a stronger signal.

To lawfully operate GMRS radios in the United States, you must get a license from the Federal Communications Commission (FCC). Everyone can use GMRS radios under the same license because it is quite easy to obtain and covers the entire family. There is no exam necessary to obtain the license, but you must pay a fee. The license is valid for ten years.

Why Choose GMRS Radio?

When considering whether to utilize a GMRS radio, it's necessary to analyze the major qualities that make it a good fit for particular scenarios. GMRS radios are preferred for their long-range capability, power, and dependability, particularly in situations when other modes of communication may fail.

Longer Range

One of the most noticeable advantages of GMRS radios is their range. FRS radios have a maximum power output of about 2 watts, but GMRS radios can transmit up to 50 watts. Because of their increased power, GMRS radios can go much further, perhaps up to 50 miles under optimum conditions. The range can vary based on geography, weather conditions, and barriers such as buildings or mountains, however, even in difficult terrain, GMRS radios outperform FRS radios. This makes GMRS an excellent alternative for outdoor excursions such as camping, trekking, or off-roading, where dependable communication is essential but cell phone coverage may be limited.

Higher Power Output

Another key consideration when adopting GMRS is its increased power output. GMRS radios can run at up to 50 watts, which is much more than other typical two-way radios, such as FRS. In contrast, FRS radios' modest power can make it difficult to sustain a signal over extended distances, particularly in locations with dense forests or steep terrain. GMRS radios, on the other hand, can overcome these obstacles, producing a far more consistent signal over longer distances. This superior power ensures that your communication is clear and uninterrupted, even when you are far away from other people or in a distant location.

Better Privacy and Less Interference

Another major aspect is privacy and the lower chance of intervention. Unlike FRS radios, GMRS radios require an FCC (Federal Communications Commission) license to operate lawfully in the United States. This implies that only licensed users are permitted to use GMRS frequencies, reducing the chance of interference from other unlicensed users, as is prevalent on the more extensively used FRS frequencies. With GMRS, you're effectively speaking in a more controlled environment, which is useful if you want to prevent interference from other users on the same frequencies.

Family Coverage with One License

If you have a family or a group of individuals who wish to use GMRS radios, there is good news: a single GMRS license can cover everyone in your home. This implies that rather than each individual requiring their own license, you can apply for a single one that is valid for everyone. This saves you time and money while also allowing you to stay connected without worrying about legal limits or additional paperwork. It's a simple method to ensure that your entire family has access to the same communication tools in the event of an emergency or for recreational purposes.

Great for Emergencies

GMRS radios are an invaluable tool in crises, particularly when traditional modes of communication, such as mobile phones, fail. When the cellular network is down or you are out of range of any cell towers, GMRS radios can let you connect with others. This is especially helpful during power outages, natural catastrophes, and other situations. Because GMRS radios do not rely on cellular networks, they provide a dependable option for remaining in touch when you need it the most. GMRS radios can also link to repeaters, which are stations designed to increase the range of your signal. These repeaters make GMRS even more useful in emergency circumstances, enabling long-distance communication when necessary.

Clearer Communication

Another benefit of GMRS is the clarity of communication. GMRS radios are noted for producing crisper sound and higher-quality communications than other types of radios that run at lesser power. This is especially critical in circumstances that need accurate communication. Whether you're providing directions on a group trek or attempting to collaborate with someone in an emergency, good communication is critical. GMRS radios are also less susceptible to static interference, which can occur with lower-power radios.

Repeaters for Extended Range

Finally, GMRS radios may link to repeaters, which are devices that magnify your radio signal and increase the range of your communications. Repeaters are extremely beneficial in locations with rugged topography, such as mountains or valleys, where the radio signal would otherwise be obscured. GMRS radios can communicate over considerably longer distances thanks to repeaters, providing you access to a wider coverage area. Many towns, particularly those with outdoor enthusiasts or emergency responders, have installed repeaters, which can improve the efficacy of GMRS radios.

To summarize, GMRS radios are an effective instrument for long-distance communication, particularly in isolated or demanding locations. Whether you use them for outdoor enjoyment, disaster preparedness, or ordinary family communication, GMRS radios provide clear, private, and efficient communication with higher power and a longer range than many other radios. If you want to use radios for anything more than simple, short-range communication, GMRS is likely worth investigating.

Who Should Use GMRS Radios?

Outdoor Enthusiasts

If you like outdoor activities such as hiking, camping, hunting, or off-roading, GMRS radios are a great option. In remote regions, there may be no cell coverage, so utilizing a GMRS radio assures that you can still communicate with your group or ask for help in the event of an emergency. GMRS radios' long-range capabilities (up to 50 miles) make them considerably more dependable than ordinary walkie-talkies or FRS radios, which have far lower ranges. So, if you're heading into the woods, GMRS radios can be a game changer.

Families

Families that love outdoor activities together or who reside in rural locations where communication can be difficult may benefit from GMRS radios. A single license covers the entire family, allowing numerous members to converse across great distances, which is especially beneficial for group events or emergencies. For example, a family trekking in the mountains can communicate even if they break off into smaller groups. If you want dependable communication for your entire home, a GMRS radio can be an excellent choice.

Preppers and Survivalists

GMRS radios are a must-have tool for anybody planning for an emergency. Whether you're preparing for a natural catastrophe, a power outage, or another type of emergency, GMRS radios let you stay connected when other communication techniques fail. Because GMRS does not rely on cellular networks, it is an ideal backup for times when cell towers are unavailable. Many preppers also utilize GMRS radios since they can connect to repeaters and communicate over longer distances. If you're planning for scenarios when every bit of communication counts, GMRS radios can help you stay connected.

Search and Rescue Teams

Search and rescue (SAR) teams utilize GMRS radios as well, particularly in remote or mountainous areas. Long-range and good communication are essential for coordinating search activities. SAR teams frequently need to communicate over great distances, even in remote or hilly places where traditional communication systems might fail. GMRS radios are dependable enough for these harsh settings, which is why they are commonly utilized in such scenarios.

RV Owners and Travelers

People who travel in RVs or other vehicles who want to drive through areas with weak cellphone service may find GMRS radios beneficial. Whether you're caravanning with other vehicles, traveling through rural areas, or touring national parks, GMRS radios keep you linked. It's also useful for talking with others in your trip party, especially if you're separated or driving in regions with no signal. Because GMRS radios can communicate over great distances, they provide better coverage in distant areas than traditional walkie-talkies or FRS radios.

Boaters

Boaters and sailors also benefit from GMRS radios, particularly while cruising in coastal or open waters. On the sea, communication can be critical, especially if something goes wrong. GMRS radios have a longer range than other maritime radios, making them excellent for bigger vessels or groups of people that are far away. These radios are ideal for communicating with your team while at sea or contacting someone on land.

People in Rural or Remote Areas

GMRS radios provide a practical alternative for remaining connected in rural locations where cell phone service can be poor or non-existent. People who reside in more remote areas can use GMRS radios to stay in touch with neighbors, friends, or family even if they are kilometers distant. Whether for ordinary communication or emergency scenarios, GMRS radios eliminate the need to rely on cell towers, which may not be available in all places.

Emergency Responders

GMRS radios are occasionally used by emergency responders, such as firemen, police, and medical teams, to coordinate in distant places. The capacity to communicate without relying on traditional infrastructure, such as cell towers or the internet, is critical in situations where existing services may be unavailable or overcrowded. GMRS radios enable rescuers to communicate in difficult situations and guarantee that everyone is on the same page, particularly when operating in big, dispersed locations.

People in Large, Spread-Out Properties

If you operate a vast property, such as a farm, ranch, or estate, GMRS radios are an excellent way to stay in touch with employees or family members. Large estates may be difficult to communicate with, especially when they are spread out throughout the country. With GMRS radios, you can stay connected over great distances without relying on mobile phones or walkie-talkies, which may have limited range. Whether you're coordinating work, tracking animals, or dealing with an emergency, GMRS radios provide a trustworthy communication option.

CHAPTER 2
GETTING STARTED WITH GMRS RADIOS

Understanding GMRS Radio Frequencies

GMRS radios use a set of frequencies in the UHF (Ultra High Frequency) band, namely between 462 MHz and 467 MHz. These frequencies are separated into channels, and each channel permits radio communication across specific distances, which vary based on the device's power output and the surroundings.

GMRS Frequency Bands

The GMRS frequency bands are often divided into two ranges:

1. 462 MHz Band.

This range has many channels, each running at a specific frequency. These are the most popular channels utilized by GMRS radios, and they serve as the principal communication channels for general usage.

2. 467 MHz Band.

This frequency range contains "repeater" channels, which help expand communication ranges. A repeater is a device that amplifies and retransmits signals across a larger region. These repeater channels can be accessible using GMRS radios, which is one of the reasons why they are so useful for long-distance communication.

GMRS frequencies are often associated with distinct channels that serve different roles. Some are for direct communication (from one radio to another), while others serve as repeaters, allowing you to converse across wider distances.

Understanding Channel Numbers

GMRS channels are normally identified with numbers ranging from 1 to 30, however, not all channels are used in all countries. Some channels are shared with other services, such as FRS, while others are specifically for GMRS usage. Channels 1-7 are frequently shared with FRS radios, however, channels 8-14 are reserved for GMRS radios. FRS and GMRS both use channels 15-22, however GMRS radios can transmit at greater power levels.

GMRS Repeater Channels

One of the most notable characteristics of GMRS is the ability to employ repeaters. A repeater works by receiving your signal, amplifying it, and then sending it out again at a higher level. This can dramatically increase the range of your transmission, allowing GMRS radios to go up to 50 miles or more, depending on terrain and weather conditions.

Repeater channels run at 467 MHz, and GMRS radios that can reach these repeater frequencies provide a substantially higher range. Using a repeater effectively doubles your communication capability, allowing you to communicate across greater distances than a traditional, direct communication link would allow. This is especially useful if you're in a low-visibility environment, such as a dense forest, or if you're operating in hilly areas where line-of-sight communication can be challenging.

Power and Frequency

The power output of GMRS radios has a considerable impact on communication efficacy. GMRS radios can transmit up to 50 watts of power, depending on the type, but FRS radios are limited to only 2 watts. The greater the power output, the further the signal can travel, which is why GMRS radios are favored for long-distance communication. Even with high power output, the radio signal can be influenced by ambient elements such as hills, buildings, or even weather. The GMRS frequencies are designed to penetrate some of these obstacles more effectively than other types of radios, although they are still limited by physical interference.

The Role of the FCC in GMRS Frequencies

In the United States, the Federal Communications Commission (FCC) regulates GMRS frequencies. To lawfully utilize GMRS frequencies, you must hold an FCC-issued license. This license enables you to transmit on GMRS frequencies while guaranteeing that your radio transmissions do not interfere with other communications in the same spectrum. The FCC licenses GMRS users to monitor radio usage and guarantee that communication is clear and uninterrupted.

It's also worth noting that the FCC has certain guidelines for how GMRS frequencies can be utilized. For example, GMRS radios must be licensed, and commercial usage of these frequencies is forbidden unless used for personal communications. Furthermore, while GMRS frequencies can be utilized by several people in the same region, the licensing system guarantees that there is some order and control over who can transmit those frequencies.

Frequency and Antenna Considerations

When it comes to GMRS radios, understanding how frequency interacts with your antenna can make a significant impact on how far your signal travels. The antenna you select for your GMRS radio has a direct influence on its range and reception quality. A decent antenna will guarantee that the radio signal is successfully broadcast and can be received over great distances, especially if you use the higher-power repeater channels. If you use the radio with a bad antenna, you may not be able to fully utilize GMRS frequencies, limiting your communication range.

Why Frequency Matters

Understanding GMRS frequencies is crucial since it allows you to tune your radio for better performance. If you understand the many channels available and their specialized applications, you can select the appropriate frequency for your purposes. For example, if you need to communicate across a longer distance, you may employ repeater channels to extend your signal's range. On the other hand, if you're conversing in a small group, you could want to use non-repeater channels for convenience.

Interference and Congestion of GMRS Frequencies

While GMRS frequencies are more tightly managed than other radio systems, there is always the danger of interference, particularly in places where numerous individuals are sharing the same frequency. Because GMRS is popular with outdoor enthusiasts, emergency responders, and others, the same frequencies may be in use simultaneously. In rare circumstances, this may result in congestion or interference. However, this can be reduced by utilizing repeaters, choosing less congested channels, or employing codes to limit the quantity of broadcast on each channel.

Types of GMRS Radios Available

When looking at GMRS radios, you will see that there are various different varieties on the market. Each kind is intended for a certain use, ranging from basic handheld radios to complex base station devices. Understanding the various varieties can help you make a better-educated decision about which GMRS radio is suitable for your requirements. Let us delve into the various varieties of GMRS radios and examine their characteristics in depth.

1. Handheld GMRS Radios

Handheld GMRS radios are the most common and widely used kind. These radios are small, portable, and simple to operate, making them perfect for everyday usage, outdoor activities, and emergency preparedness. Handheld GMRS radios are lightweight and can be carried easily in a backpack or attached to a belt, providing users with a great lot of flexibility and mobility.

Features:

- **Portability**: Handheld radios are small and easy to carry. They are perfect for individuals who need communication during outdoor adventures like hiking, camping, or off-roading.
- **Power Output**: Most handheld GMRS radios operate at a power output of 1 to 5 watts. While this is not as high as mobile radios or base stations, it's still sufficient for short to medium-range communication, especially in open areas with few obstructions.
- **Range**: The range typically varies from a few miles up to 20 miles, depending on environmental factors like terrain, weather conditions, and the power of the radio.
- **Rechargeable Batteries**: Handheld radios often use rechargeable batteries, which can be convenient for users who need long-term use. Some models may also use standard AA or AAA batteries for backup.
- **Ease of Use**: These radios typically feature a simple interface with easy-to-read displays and large buttons, making them user-friendly for a wide range of people.

Best For:

Handheld GMRS radios are ideal for individuals, families, and small groups who require basic communication over medium distances. They are great for outdoor enthusiasts who require communication when hiking through the bush, as well as explorers who need to stay in contact while participating in off-road activities. They're also handy in emergencies, especially if you're in a region with little or no cell phone coverage.

2. Mobile GMRS Radios

Mobile GMRS radios are intended for use in vehicles including automobiles, trucks, RVs, and boats. These radios are normally located on the dashboard or within the car and require an external power source, which is usually provided by the vehicle's electrical system. Mobile GMRS radios are more powerful than handheld ones, providing longer range and more consistent communication in certain situations.

Features:

- **Higher Power Output**: Mobile GMRS radios often have a higher power output, typically ranging from 5 to 50 watts. This allows them to communicate over longer distances compared to handheld radios, often reaching up to 50 miles in ideal conditions.
- **Improved Range**: Thanks to their higher power output and the elevated position of the antenna (mounted on top of the vehicle), mobile radios can achieve much greater communication distances. This is especially helpful in rural or mountainous areas where signal blockage from terrain can affect other types of radios.
- **External Antenna**: One of the key features of mobile radios is the ability to connect to an external antenna. A high-quality external antenna significantly improves signal reception and transmission, increasing the radio's range and clarity.

- **Advanced Features**: Mobile GMRS radios usually come with more advanced features, such as multiple channels, weather alerts, and the ability to connect to repeaters for an extended communication range.
- **Mounting**: These radios are typically mounted in a vehicle, so they're not as portable as handheld radios. However, they're designed for constant use in situations where you need reliable communication while on the road or at sea.

Best For:

Mobile GMRS radios are ideal for those who want long-range communication while traveling or driving a vehicle. They're great for RV owners, truck drivers, off-road enthusiasts, and boaters who need to keep connected while traveling. They're also useful in emergency scenarios where you need dependable communication gear in your car, or while coordinating with a group in remote locations.

3. Base Station GMRS Radios

Base station GMRS radios are more powerful and advanced than portable and mobile radios. These are commonly utilized in permanent sites, such as houses, offices, or other structures, where continual, dependable communication is required. Base stations are meant to remain stationary while providing additional power and range, making them ideal for emergency preparedness or communication over vast distances.

Features:

- **High Power Output**: Base station radios typically offer the highest power output, often up to 50 watts. This allows them to communicate over very long distances, making them the go-to option for users who need maximum range.
- **Stationary Setup**: Since base station radios are fixed in one location, they require an external power source, often from an AC power outlet, rather than relying on batteries. These radios also use an external antenna, which can be mounted on a roof or a high structure for the best signal.
- **Great for Communication Over Large Areas**: Base station radios are perfect for people who need to communicate with others over long distances or across large areas. For example, they're often used in rural areas, where residents may need to stay in contact with neighbors, family members, or local emergency services.
- **Advanced Features**: These radios are generally packed with features such as built-in repeaters, scanning capabilities, and weather alert notifications. They are more suited to those who require constant, reliable communication, especially in professional settings.
- **Stationary Location**: Since they are designed for use in one place, base station radios aren't as portable as handheld radios. They're best suited for people who need to have constant communication from a fixed location.

Best For:

Base station GMRS radios are appropriate for users who want strong, long-range communication from a fixed position. They're widely utilized by rural or isolated families, emergency services, and company owners who need to communicate constantly. They're also ideal for preppers or survivalists who need a dependable communication tool that can cover large distances in the event of a crisis.

4. GMRS Radios with Repeaters

While not a unique category, GMRS radios built to function with repeaters demand special attention. Repeaters increase the range of GMRS radios by receiving a weak signal and retransmitting it at a higher strength, allowing communication over longer distances than a single radio could do alone.

Features:

- **Extended Range**: Repeaters can dramatically extend the range of GMRS radios, allowing communication over 50 miles or more. By using repeaters, GMRS radios can bypass obstacles like mountains or buildings, improving the overall communication quality.
- **Two-Way Communication**: Using repeaters doesn't mean you're limited to one-way communication. Repeaters allow for full-duplex communication, meaning you can talk and listen without switching modes, just like on a phone.
- **Installation and Setup**: Setting up a repeater usually involves a more complex installation process, which might require specialized

knowledge, but once installed, it provides a reliable long-range communication option.

Best For:

GMRS radios with repeaters are ideal for users who need to communicate over large distances, particularly in places with rough terrain or dense populations where direct communication may be ineffective. They are widely utilized by emergency services, preppers, and big groups that require reliable communication across great distances.

Required Licenses and Regulations

The FCC gives people special permission called a GMRS license that lets them talk back and forth using GMRS frequencies. It's needed because GMRS radios use more power (up to 50 watts) than other radios, like FRS radios. Because of this, they need to be controlled so they don't mess up other contact services. Anyone who wants to transmit on GMRS frequencies needs to have a license, which is usually good for 10 years from the date it was issued.

The person who wants to get a GMRS license doesn't have to take a written test like they do for many other FCC licenses. Instead, you have to pay a fee and give some general details as part of the application process. This information helps the FCC make sure that GMRS frequencies are used in a smart way that doesn't interfere with other services. But it's important to know that GMRS licenses can't be given to someone else. This means that if you sell your radio or give it to someone else, the new owner will need to apply for their own license.

Who Needs a GMRS License?

Anyone, including families, who wants to use GMRS radios needs to get a license. Among these are:

- **Individuals**: You need a license to use a GMRS radio, whether it's a pocket or a cell phone. The license covers all personal uses of GMRS frequencies, such as talking to family or friends while camping, in an emergency, or just while doing fun things outside.

- **Families**: All members of your direct family can use the same GMRS license. In other words, everyone in your home can properly use GMRS radios since you only need one license. The license, on the other hand, only covers your family. Anyone else who wants to use GMRS frequencies would need their own permission.

- **Businesses and Organizations**: GMRS is mostly for personal use, but some businesses or organizations may also need a license to use GMRS radios for non-business reasons. A group might use GMRS radios to plan actions across a big area, and the group's leader would need to have a GMRS license.

How to Obtain a GMRS License

Step 1. Register for a Username

Note: If you have already signed up for CORES, you can skip this step.

You can register for an FCC login by going to the FCC Universal License System (ULS) page and clicking on "**New User Registration**" under "**Filing**." This link will take you to the page where you can sign in to your FCC account. Then, click on the "**Register**" button next to "**Need a Username?**" This link will take you to the online form to sign up for the FRN.

Before you fill out the form, you will need to make sure that you are not already registered. Click "**Check Availability**" and type in your email address. This will be the name you use. Watch the last few minutes of this movie and follow the steps there to get back your old password if you can't remember your email address.

If your email or account isn't already there, go to the form and fill it out. Fill out the form with your name and address. Then choose a password. The FCC says that the password needs to have at least one number, one capital letter, one small letter, and one punctuation mark or other special symbol. Also, it needs to be 12 to 15 letters long.

Next, choose a security question, type in an answer, and click "**Submit**." Your email address and username will need to be checked after the form is sent.

Click the "**GoToCores**" button to move on to step 2, where you will need to sign up for a FRN number.

Step 2. Register for an FRN number.

Note: You can skip this step if you already have a FRN number.

You will need a FRN, which stands for "**FCC Registration Number**," before you can apply for any FCC license. When you do business with the FCC, they will use your FRN, which is a 10-digit number, to find you. The IRS knows that you work if you have a social security number, and the FCC knows that you pay fees if you have a FRN. The form will also need your SSN, so be ready for that.

Don't forget that your FRN will be needed for all apps, changes, refills, and upgrades to your license. Your FRN number will never change.

You can also go to the FCC Universal License System (ULS) page, click on "**Filing**," and then enter your username and password under "**Username Login**," which will take you to the User Home page after you complete Step 1.

Now things start to get interesting. This page will give you the following six choices:

- **Associate Username to FRN**: Connect your registered username to a current FRN.
- **Manage Existing FRNs | FRN Financial | Bills and Fees**: You can view and pay regulatory fees, application fees, and bills, as well as see the red and green light state for existing FRNs.
- **Register New FRN:** Sign up for a new FRN and get it, which may include a Restricted Use FRN.
- **Reset FRN Password:** Change or reset your FRN password.
- **Search for FRN:** Look for information about the FRN that is available to the public.
- **Update your username profile**.

You can go straight to step 3 if you have a FRN. The third item is "**Register New FRN**." Clicking on it will bring up a box with radio buttons that let us select how to register.

People can register for either a personal or a business reason. A GMRS license can't be given to a business, so you should choose "An Individual." This is the right choice because your contact address should be in the US or one of its areas. Click on "**Continue**."

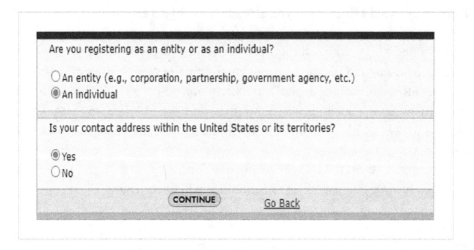

This will take you to a different box with more radio buttons. Select **CORES FRN Registration** and click **Continue**.

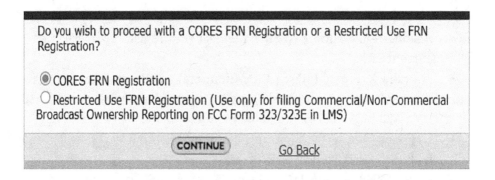

This link will take you to the real FRN sign-up form online. Yes, one more form. Fill out the form with your name and address.

FRN Registration

Register a Domestic Individual			
Salutation:	[▾]	First Name: *	[ ]
Middle Initial:	[ ]	Last Name: *	[ ]
Suffix:	[ ]	Doing Business As:	[ ]

If you have a Social Security Number or Taxpayer Identification Number, enter and confirm it here.

SSN:	[ ]	Confirm SSN:	[ ]

If you do not have a Social Security Number, select a reason: [▾] [?]

Contact Information			
Same as Above:	☐		
Organization:	[ ]	Position:	[ ]
Salutation:	[▾]	First Name: *	[ ]
Middle Initial:	[ ]	Last Name: *	[ ]
Suffix:	[ ]		
Address Line 1: *	[ ]	Address Line 2:	[ ]
City: *	[ ]	State: *	ALABAMA [▾]
Zip Code: *	[ ] [ ]	Phone:	[ ] [ ] ext. [ ]
Fax:	[ ] [ ]	Email: *	[ ]

(SUBMIT)   Go Back

Asterisks (*) indicate required fields.

Revised: April 2005   Form 160 - Approved by OMB 3060-0917

NOTICE TO INDIVIDUALS REQUIRED BY THE PRIVACY ACT OF 1974 AND THE PAPERWORK REDUCTION ACT OF 1995

After you send and receive the form, you should be taken to a page with information about your FRN register. The FRN number you were given should be at the top of the box. Keep this number safe so you can find it again later. You worked really hard to get this number.

Important side note: You need to connect your FRNs to your username before you can use them. Go back to the User Home page and click on Associate Username to FRN. Then, fill out the short form that comes up.

Step 3. Apply for the license

You can begin the process of getting a license once you have your FRN number. To file online, go to the FCC Universal License System (ULS) page and click on "**File**." This should take you to a page where you can sign in to License Manager. Type in your new FRN number and password to get in.

Click on **"Apply for a New License"** on the left side of the page that says "**My Licenses**." This will take you to a new page with a drop-down choice where you can pick the service license you need. You will want to choose **ZA**, which stands for "**General Mobile Radio (GMRS).**" On the next page, there will be three drop-down options. You will be led to, you guessed it, another form after clicking "Continue" and then "Continue Again." Once you send that one, you should be taken to a page where you can handle FRNs that are already in your account.

This page has a lot of words in red that look scary, and we can do one of four things:

- Manage FRNs
- FRN Financial
- Regulatory Fee Manager
- ULS Pay Fees

You thought you were done? Not really. Now is the time to pay the fee. Any website would make these steps simple to understand and carry out. They have finished the entry process. When you click "Pay," the application is over. But this page is different from others. It's up to the FCC. This makes it seem like it must be way too hard in every way. We have already filled out two forms with mostly the same information. We are now going to a different part of the FCC website.

Step 4. Pay the license application fee

Pick FRN Financial from the list of FRNs you already own and run. This link will take you to the page where you can pay the fee. To the left of your FRN number should be a link that says "**View/Make Payments**." If you click on that link, you'll be taken to a new page where your FRN is listed under the tab that says "**Awaiting Payment Confirmation**." On that page, there is a link that says "**Make Payment**." Click on that link, fill out the payment form, and send it. You're done now.

The FCC should give you your GMRS name in a few days. You can check your license and name in the ULS License Manager by logging in.

GMRS Regulations and Usage Rules

It's important to know how to use GMRS radios properly once you have your license. These rules help keep things running smoothly and avoid getting in the way of other services. These are the most important rules to follow:

1. License Required for Transmission: As we already said, anyone using GMRS radios needs to have a current FCC license. For me, this is the most important rule. If you are caught broadcasting without a license, you might have to pay a fine.

2. No Commercial Use: GMRS can only be used for personal, non-business purposes. Of course, this means you can't use GMRS radios for business, like to keep track of workers or make money. GMRS is not the same as commercial radio services that companies, first responders, and public safety groups use. If you need to use radios for business, you may need to get a different license or use a service like the Business Radio Service.

3. Power Capacity: GMRS radios can transmit with up to 50 watts of power, which is more than many other types of radios. So, this power limit is very strict. It's important to stay within the acceptable power range when using your GMRS radio so that you don't mess up other people's conversations.

4. Radio Equipment Standards: The FCC has set clear rules for the kinds of radios that can work on GMRS frequencies. To make sure they work right and don't cause damaging interference, these radios have to meet certain technical requirements. Before you buy a GMRS radio, make sure that the company that made it has approved it for use with GMRS.

5. Channel Use and Frequency Allocation: GMRS radios use certain frequencies that are also used by other radio systems, such as FRS (Family Radio Service). It's important to know the frequency assignments and which channels are used for GMRS and FRS, even though GMRS has its own set of channels and some are shared with FRS. Most of the time, you can use GMRS channels with higher power settings. Just be careful not to bother people who are using FRS radios on the same channels.

6. Public Safety: Even if you don't have an FCC license, you can use GMRS radios for public safety contact without any problems. You are permitted to transmit on GMRS frequencies in a genuine situation to ask for assistance or alert other people to danger. Normal working rules should be followed again, though, once the situation is over.

7. No Public Broadcasts: GMRS radios can't be used to transmit music, news, or entertainment material to the general public. They can only be used for two-way conversations between approved users.

8. Repeater Use: GMRS radios can interact with repeaters, which are gadgets that transmit signals to increase the range of contact. It is important to use the correct repeater frequencies if you want to use a repeater. These frequencies are usually in the 467 MHz area. You should also check to see if your radio can connect to repeaters since not all GMRS radios can do this.

Penalties for Violating GMRS Regulations

If you don't follow the rules set by GMRS, there could be bad results. Fines are one of the punishments the FCC can give for illegal broadcasts. Here are some of the most usual violations:

- **Operating without a license**: If you are caught transmitting on GMRS frequencies without a valid license, you could be fined and required to cease transmission.
- **Interference with other communications**: If your radio causes interference with other services, such as emergency communications or other licensed users, the FCC can issue fines or require you to cease operating your radio.
- **Commercial use**: Using GMRS radios for business purposes or commercial activities can result in penalties and a loss of your license.

CHAPTER 3

SETTING UP YOUR GMRS RADIO

GMRS Radio Installation

TOOLS:

- 10MM socket
- Ratchet wrench
- Step drill bit (minimum 7/8 – 1-1/8) or a 1-1/8 drill bit
- Drill
- Flathead screwdriver or plastic pry tool
- Wire crimping tool
- Wire stripping tool
- Heat gun or torch
- Dremel w/ plastic cutting blade
- Fish tape or a wire hanger
- Stubby Phillips head screwdriver

These are the thorough steps that I am giving for installing your GMRS radio in their 4Runner. If you already have all of the parts and instruments, read them carefully.

Step 1: Disconnect the Power

First, let's talk about being safe. You will turn off the power to your car at the start of this process, just like you would before doing any other kind of work on your car.

It was clear to me that I wanted all of the wires to be under the glove box in this circumstance. This means that you will need to move the knee airbag on the passenger side of your fifth-generation Land Rover 4Runner. First, I turned off the power, and then I took down the panels themselves.

Step 2: Take Off the Panels

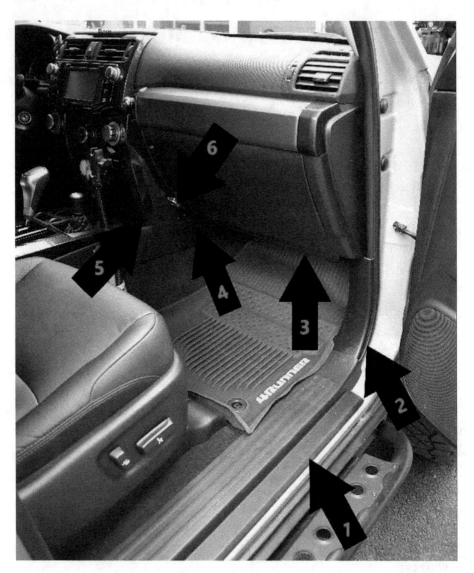

After that, I took off the passenger side kick panel and the other pieces that went with it. To get to one of the three bolts that hold the airbag in place, you will need to take off a small cover on the lower left side of the bottom of the glove drawer. This cover is on the left side of the bottom of the glove box. I chose to put the RJ45 coupler here, so it's important to have this little cover handy.

Step 3: Move the Airbag

After taking off all of the panels, you will now have access to the three 10mm bolts that hold the knee airbag in place on the passenger side of the car. In order to pop each clip one by one, I found that it worked best to start on the door side and work my way toward the middle of the car. The knee airbag on the passenger side is held in place by three bolts. Once you have removed them, you will need to pull on it because it is attached to the bottom of the glove box with plastic clips.

I did not take the airbag off the car after it was deactivated. Since I don't like to play with airbags, I moved it and put it in the footwell, where no one would touch it.

Step 4: Take the Glove Box Off

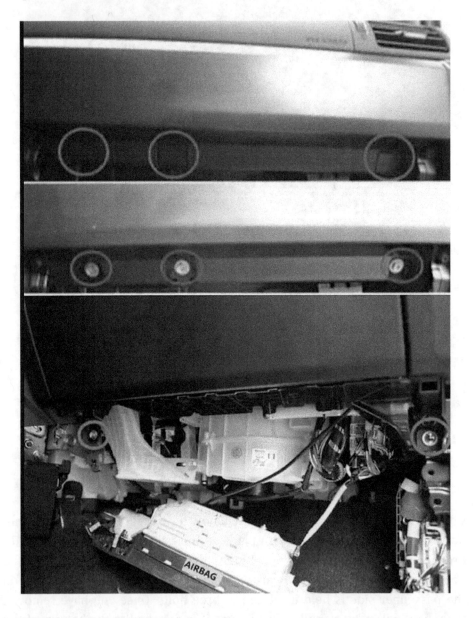

Moving the airbag out of the way will let you reach the two 10mm bolts that hold the glove box's bottom in place. You can now take these nuts off for your own comfort. Pulling the glove box out will let you get to the three plastic covers that are covering the three top mounting nuts.

You can do this with either your flat head or your plastic pry tool. After the fastening nuts are loose, you should be able to easily take off the glove box by pulling on both the top and bottom at the same time. The wire for your glove box light is held in place by a pair of plastic clips. If you press the sides of the clips into place and take off the light, you can take the glove box off the car completely. You will have more space to work with after this.

Step 5: Outfit Glove Box With Outlets

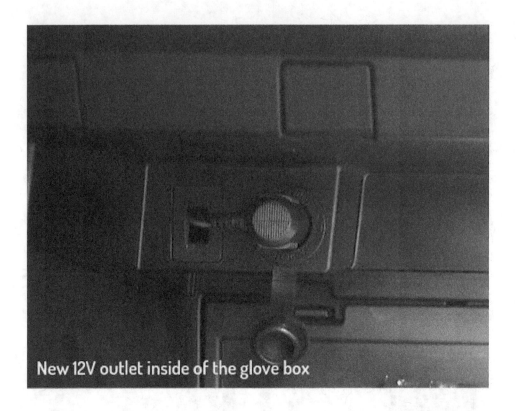

New 12V outlet inside of the glove box

Now that I have everything out of the glove box, we can put it back together and get it ready.

On the left side of the glove box, there is a round cover that looks like a 12V plug and a rectangle cover. These two plates are both on the left side. They both have tabs on the back that you will need to push on in order to take them off. You can take off both covers. The round cover can be thrown away or kept since the Blue Seas 12V plug will be put there instead. On the other hand, you will need to keep the rectangle cover.

After taking off the covers, you will need to use the 1-1/8-inch drill bit or the step bit to drill out the circle hole so that the 12V Blue Seas outlet can fit. Just a little drilling will be enough to make room for the outlet. After the hole has been drilled, put it in the Blue Seas exit.

You can now take off the square cover and use a Dremel to make a hole for the Midland MXT275's 12V power socket. The MicroMobile power plug has a disconnect, so the pass-through only needs to be big enough to fit the link. You can easily take apart and put back together the inline fuse after the pass-through you cut out is finished. Following that, make sure the 12V socket is plugged in through the square cover that is connected to the glove box.

Step 6: Run Power to Outlet

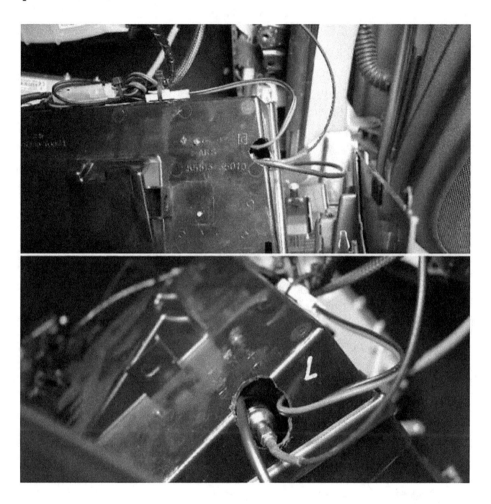

Before you can move forward, you will need to figure out how you are going to power the 12V outlet. I needed a plug that was always on so that I could power the radio whenever we needed to. It was also important to have an extra 12-volt power outlet for when I was not using the GMRS radio.

I was able to get power from the place where our car already had an electricity tray unit installed, which can hold a Blue Seas 6 circuit switch block. The Power Tray had the necessary breaker for the 12V plug, but I still had to make the microphone line longer.

The next step was to figure out how long my lines should be by measuring them based on where my fuse block was. After that, I sheathed our cords. It was the #8 nylon insulated ring connections that I used to connect to the fuse block. It is important to remember that the power is still off.

Then, I used fish tape to wrap the positive and negative lines around the back firewall and through the main hole on the firewall on the passenger side. You should try to pull the radio cord and the wires through at the same time if you can. I put everything in place by connecting a crimped 12-10 AWG female completely insulated nylon disconnect to the back of our 12V plug. This was done after the wires were passed through the firewall in the way I wanted.

I will still be working on the glove box, so don't put it together or connect anything else just yet.

Step 7: Mount the Antenna

There is no hard and fast rule for where to put the antenna; the user is the only one who can decide. I chose the hood. If you do too, make sure the mount doesn't rub against the fender and the set screws are tight.

If you haven't already, you will put the cable through the same hole that you used for the wires. Then, you can secure the cable however you like. You will need to pull the extra cable through the hole, bundle it up nicely, make sure it is safe from anything that could pinch it, and then tuck it under the glove box when you are done changing the wire.

Step 8: Mount and Connect the Main Unit

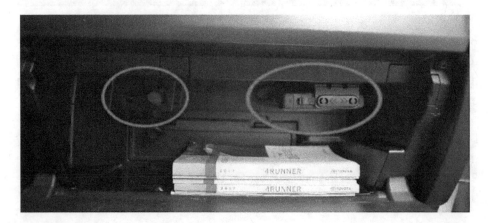

Going to the next step, which is putting the main unit, you can choose where to put it inside the glove box. The Midland main unit comes with mounting tools and a mount to make sure it is in place firmly. I wanted to keep the main unit out of the way and out of sight so that the panel would look clean and there would be as few wires as possible that could be seen.

The radio cable, power cable, and 3' Cat.5E cable could all fit through the hole I drilled in the glove box's right side. After that, I drilled a hole big enough for the connections to stick out of. This would allow the main unit to be placed flat against the side of the glove box. It would also keep the cables and wires from being visible from inside the glove since they came from the back of the unit.

I used a short Phillips head screwdriver and the hardware that was given to us to connect the mount for the main unit after putting the glove box light back in place and moving the clips that were holding the wires in place.

Step 9: Connect the Antenna Cable and Power Wires

The radio cord was the first thing I connected. Then I connected the power wire for the main unit to the wires for the glove box light. After that, I hooked up the positive and negative lines to the right places on the back of the 12V plug. It's important to make sure that all of the links are sealed and heat-shrunk.

Step 10: Install Coupler for The Mic

You can connect the Cat.5E cable to the front of the main unit after connecting the power to the 12V outlet, the antenna wire to the back of the main unit, and the power to the main unit. For the three-foot wire to work, you will need to put it through the same hole as the antenna and other connections. Next, put the glovebox and airbag back in the car in the opposite order of how you removed them.

Run the Cat.5E wire down and over the back of the airbag to get to where the RJ45 coupler will be put in. Then, take the small cover that was on top of the bolt that I took off at the start of the process. Find the spot where you want to put your RJ45 Coupler using your step bit again, and then carefully drill the hole so that it can fit the coupler.

The given hardware should be used to hold the coupler in place, the Cat.5E wire should be connected to the back, and the cover should be put back on the car while making sure it fits correctly.

Step 11: Reattach Panels and Install Mic Mount

Without Handheld Mic

With Handheld Mic

After this is done, clean the area and then put back on the car all the parts that were taken off in the opposite order. It is very important to make sure that the antenna is attached to the mount before you connect the mobile unit to the RJ45 connection. Check that the mobile device is charged and that it works properly as well.

It was clear when I pressed the weather button and looked again to make sure. This means you can now put your Nite Ize plate anywhere you want. The microphone clip was on the back of the portable device. I switched it out for the flat part of the Nite Ize mount. After that, I put a small amount of RTV on the base to make sure it wouldn't come loose. You might also want to buy a cover for the radio mount if you plan to take it off and put it back on more than once.

This is the end of the installation process for the GMRS radio. You can now leave it out while you use it or put it away when you go to the store.

Setting Up a GMRS Repeater

Requirements for setting up a GMRS repeater

There are various requirements for setting up a GMRS repeater. In the following, I have mentioned these:

1. **License:** In the United States, a valid General Mobile Radio Service (GMRS) license issued by the Federal Communications Commission (FCC) is required.
2. **Two GMRS transceivers:** Two GMRS transceivers, one of which will function as the receiver and the other of which will send and receive signals.
3. **A Duplexer:** An antenna duplexer is a device that enables the receiver and the transmitter to use the same antenna while also preventing interference between the two radio frequencies.
4. **An Antenna:** An antenna is a device that is used for the purpose of transmitting and receiving radio waves. The particular application and the area where the repeater is being set up will both play a role in determining the sort of antenna that is placed in use.
5. **A Power supply:** This is what is utilized to deliver power to the transceivers and any other electronic equipment that is linked with them.

6. **A Control System:** A system that is used to govern the functioning of the repeater, including the ability to switch the transmitter on and off, alter the power level, and add the appropriate tones or codes to the signal.
7. **A Suitable Location:** The repeater has to be situated in a location where it can successfully receive and send signals. It's possible that this is on a tower, rooftop, or some other elevated site.

It is also crucial to remember that the equipment for the GMRS repeater should be installed and maintained by a qualified technician in compliance with the FCC's guidelines.

How to Set Up A GMRS Repeater

There are several steps involved in putting up a GMRS repeater, and it is critical to have a thorough understanding of the technique before attempting to build one.

A complete summary of the technique is provided below:

- Gather needed equipment, including two GMRS transceivers, a duplexer, an antenna, a power supply, and a control system. Everything I have spoken in the past.
- Identify a suitable location for the repeater. It is critical that this position be raised so that the repeater can properly receive and transmit communication signals.
- After installing the antenna, connect it to the GMRS duplexer. This will guarantee that the broadcast and receive signals remain unique while also avoiding interference.
- Connect the duplexer to both the receiver and transmitter, as well as the power supply for the control system and transceivers.
- Check and adjust repeater control system settings as needed. This will entail not just configuring the repeater to broadcast and receive on the correct frequencies, but also determining any tone or code requirements that may be necessary.
- To ensure proper functionality, test the repeater by transmitting and receiving signals.

Before attempting to set up a GMRS repeater, make sure you understand how it works.

How does a GMRS Repeater Work?

A General Mobile Radio Service (GMRS) repeater works by receiving radio signals at a certain frequency and retransmitting them at the same or other frequency.

As a result, transmissions can travel a greater distance than they would with a single radio. A General Mobile Radio Service (GMRS) radio transmits a signal on a certain frequency, which is picked up by the repeater's antenna.

- The repeater's receiver then receives the signal and amplifies it.
- After being amplified, the signal is passed through a duplexer, which separates the signals being sent and received to prevent interference.
- The signal is subsequently transferred to the repeater's transmitter, which retransmits it on a different frequency or at the same frequency as the original broadcast.
- The retransmitted signal is then picked up by longer-range GMRS radios, allowing them to connect with the radio that made the original transmission.

In addition, the General Mobile Radio Service (GMRS) repeater will be outfitted with a control system that will manage the repeater's operations. This system will control the power level, turn on and off the transmitter, and add the necessary tones or codes to the signal.

How to Connect to GMRS Repeater

1. Determine the frequency of the repeater with which you want to connect. In most situations, this information can be acquired on the repeater's website or by contacting the repeater's administrators.
2. Set the frequency on your GMRS radio according to the instructions. In most situations, this will include programming the frequency into the radio's memory and, if necessary, setting the tone or code required to access the repeater.

3. Activate your radio and tune it to the channel or frequency you programmed in step two.
4. While you're waiting for the repeater's access tone or code to play, hit the push-to-talk button on your radio and listen to the sound.
5. Once the access tone or code has been triggered, speak clearly and concisely, explaining your destination and callsign.
6. After you've released the push-to-talk button, wait for the other person to respond.
7. You are now connected to the repeater and can communicate with other radios that are also connected to it.

It is important to note that certain repeaters may have particular limits on access and use, such as time-slot or time-out intervals. Before attempting to connect to the repeater, it is critical to establish whether these restrictions are in place.

Use a GMRS Repeater for Longer Range

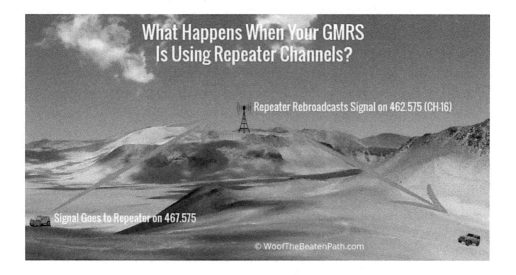

What Do You Need to Use a GMRS Repeater?

To utilize a GMRS repeater, your radio must have this capability. Both portable GMRS radios, such as the Baofeng UV-9G, and fixed-mount mobiles, such as the Midland MXT-500 and MXT-575, offer repeater functionality. Because repeater programming varies by model, we will not go into depth on how to configure your GMRS radio to use repeaters; nonetheless, the basic principle is as follows:

In most circumstances, a GMRS radio capable of repeater operation will already have channels configured for this purpose. These channels can be adjusted using either the radio's front panel or a programming connection and computer. On the receiving side, the repeater channels correspond to the eight high-power GMRS channels (15-22), however, when you utilize them, your radio transmits at a frequency five megahertz higher.

It is possible that you will hear communication from a repeater on those conventional channels; but, in order to use the repeater, you must switch to the channel that corresponds to the repeater and maybe enter special tones to activate the machine. It is not difficult to set up these elements if you have a basic comprehension of them, despite the fact that they may appear complex in general.

How Do You Use a GMRS Repeater for Longer Range?

When we use our radios in a usual fashion, such as when we communicate with other members of our group on channel 16, we transmit and receive on the same frequency or channel. The word for this mode is simplex mode. Our signal just evaporates from the antenna and goes in the direction of the person we wish to connect with, assuming they are within range. It is conceivable that we will be unable to speak with them if the distance between us is too vast or there is something obstructing our signal, such as a mountain.

When GMRS repeaters first appeared, they functioned similarly to cell towers and relay stations. They were able to pick up and transmit our signal further than was previously possible. Some GMRS repeaters cover hundreds of square miles and are commonly located on mountain peaks, like the 462.600 machine near Silverton, Colorado.

How Do Repeaters Work

This relaying technique cannot be performed on the same frequency without causing interference; hence, the repeater "listens" to a second radio frequency five megahertz higher than the one we are now listening to. When you transmit on a repeater channel, your radio's signal is transmitted on a frequency that only the repeater can receive before being repeated on the normal frequency, which in this case is channel 16.

All of this switching will take place automatically if you select one of the repeater channels on GMRS radios that are "repeater capable."

How to Find and Ask for Permission to Use GMRS Repeaters

The great majority of GMRS repeaters are owned by local communities or individuals, and not all of them are open to the public. MyGMRS.com is one of the best websites for finding and learning how to utilize local GMRS repeaters. This website has an interactive map that displays contact information, state (open repeater, private, permission required, etc.), and any tones required to access the repeater.

MyGMRS.com is another great site. You can also search the internet for local repeater organizations and request access to the computers they control. MyGMRS.com is only one choice. Before utilizing your repeater-capable GMRS, you should always check its ownership status, especially if it is attached to a repeater.

What are the GMRS Repeater Tones?

Many repeaters employ CTCSS tones to control access and prevent the machine from broadcasting signals that are not necessary. It is very likely that you will need to set a privacy tone for the repeater channel that you intend to utilize on your radio. If you do not accomplish this, the repeater will not respond to your queries. There is a good chance that there are many repeaters in the same area, and they may even be using the same channel, but not the same access tones. For this reason, it is advantageous to own a radio that allows you to build multiple do-it-yourself unique channels.

In addition, there are repeaters that broadcast a CTCSS tone to the receiver. If you just want to receive signals coming from that specific repeater, you can use this tone to your advantage. In addition, some repeater owners are now employing DCS (digital coded squelch) instead of CTCSS. The core notion remains the same, with the distinction that DCS uses a digital signal rather than an analog tone. Most latest mobile GMRS radios and handhelds can send both CTCSS tones and DCS-coded signals.

Open Repeaters and the 141.3 Hz GMRS Travel Tone

When we receive a new GMRS radio and program it using Chirp, we first set all of the repeater channels to generate a 141.3 Hz CTCSS tone. This is among the first things we do. To get access to "open repeaters," which utilize the informal GMRS "travel tone" of 141.3 Hz, this level of tone is commonly used. It is not true that all repeaters that use this tone are considered "open." Before you start conversing on the system you're using, make sure it's open to everyone.

Power Source and Battery Management

Power Source:

GMRS radios typically use one of two types of power sources: rechargeable batteries or disposable batteries. These two sorts of batteries provide the foundation of effective communication in a variety of situations. To choose amongst these choices, consider the user's preferences, environmental conditions, and the desired balance of convenience and long-term expenses.

- **Rechargeable Batteries**: General Mobile Radio Service (GMRS) radios often make use of the adaptability offered by rechargeable batteries, particularly Nickel Metal Hydride (NiMH) or Lithium-ion (Li-ion) kinds of batteries. They can go through numerous cycles of recharging, which is a significant benefit since it provides an alternative to throwaway batteries that is both environmentally friendly and economically viable. Those consumers who are looking for economic efficiency, as well as decreased environmental effects, are likely to find this environmentally friendly method appealing.
- **Disposable Batteries**: As an alternative, GMRS radios are equipped to handle disposable batteries, which offers a handy power option for users who may not have access to charging facilities. As a result of this flexibility, users can modify their power source in accordance with the resources that are available, which lends GMRS radios the capacity to adapt to a wide range of circumstances.

Battery Life:

The battery life of any GMRS radio system is its most critical metric, and it is directly related to usage patterns, power settings, and the type of batteries used. Despite the fact that rechargeable batteries have a shorter lifetime for a single use than disposable batteries, they frequently demonstrate their value over time by being less expensive and capable of being recharged.

Charging Considerations

To effectively navigate the world of charging, users are strongly advised to rigorously adhere to the manufacturer's instructions. Overcharging rechargeable batteries can lower their overall lifetime, which can be troublesome. The charging infrastructure, which frequently takes the form of desktop chargers or USB charging alternatives, is intended to make charging more convenient for consumers by allowing them to select charging locations based on their preferences.

Backup Power

Backup power solutions should be included in the GMRS radio user's toolbox since they are prudent. When traveling for an extended period of time, it may be impractical to rely on a single power source. As a result, having backup batteries or different power sources is critical to ensuring constant communication during travel.

Low Battery Indicators

GMRS radios provide low battery indications, which are an essential component of the complicated dance that is power management. These modest but important signals alert users when the energy reserve is about to be drained. They serve as a timely warning to take preventive measures, such as replacing or charging the battery, to avoid communication disruptions.

External Power Options

The usage of external power choices allows the experienced GMRS radio enthusiast an additional level of freedom. Extending the operational lifetime of GMRS radios through the use of car adapters and external battery packs is extremely advantageous, especially when traveling for extended periods of time or in situations where regular recharge is not feasible.

Within the context of GMRS radio operation, having a thorough understanding of the complexities involved in power source selection and battery management not only improves the user experience but also ensures a smooth and reliable communication channel in a variety of different contexts. Always refer to the user manual for instructions specific to your GMRS radio model. This will allow you to fully utilize the capabilities of these crucial communication devices.

GPS Integration and Location Services

GPS Integration:

General Mobile Radio Service (GMRS) radios with GPS technology employ satellite-based positioning systems to determine and transmit the user's geographic coordinates. This new feature makes GMRS radios more functional, resulting in a wide range of benefits, including the following:

- ***Precise Location Information:*** GMRS radios that are equipped with GPS technology provide users with precise location data in real-time.

Utilizing this function is quite beneficial when it comes to properly reacting to crises, identifying members of the team, and arranging activities for groups.

- **Navigation and Wayfinding**: Users can make use of the built-in navigation and wayfinding tools, which make use of the GPS data to plan routes, establish waypoints, and navigate across terrain that is foreign to them. This proves to be very beneficial while carrying out activities that take place outside, such as hiking, camping, or off-road excursions.
- **Emergency Situations**: The Global Positioning System (GPS) feature becomes a vital resource in the event of an emergency scenario. Whether it's search and rescue operations or cooperating with emergency services, the transmission of exact position information during times of emergency helps to make response activities more expedient and effective.

Location Services:

In addition to GPS coordinates, GMRS radios that can provide advanced location services offer a comprehensive range of features that can enhance user experiences. These features include the following:

- Certain GMRS radios have mapping and geofencing capabilities, allowing users to view their location on digital maps. Geofencing is another function that may be included with these radios. Geofencing systems improve security and coordination by allowing users to define virtual borders and get warnings when those limits are breached.
- Real-time location sharing fosters collaboration and coordination among users. This capacity is especially useful when teams are distributed over large regions or are working on activities that need coordinated efforts.
- GMRS radios may record location history data, allowing users to review their journeys. This option allows you to review prior routes, analyze activities, and optimize future planning.

Privacy and Security Considerations

Although there are obvious benefits to integrating GPS and location services, it is critical to consider privacy and security concerns. GMRS radios with these features frequently have settings that allow users to control the sharing of location information. This allows users to have control over their personal privacy.

RF Interference Mitigation Strategies

To guarantee that GMRS radios continue to deliver clear and reliable communication, interference from radio frequency (RF) must be reduced. Communication transmissions may be affected by radio frequency interference, which can come from a variety of sources. Efficient mitigation solutions are critical for achieving optimal performance. Here are a few methods for reducing RF interference:

- **Frequency Selection**: First, select a frequency or channel that is clear and has low congestion. Check to discover if there are any local limits or requirements for the usage of GMRS frequencies. It is preferable to avoid frequencies that are often impacted by interference in your specific area.
- **Antenna Placement and Orientation**: Make sure the radio's antenna is positioned and orientated optimally. If it is an external antenna, ensure that it is fully extended. Experiment with different places to find which one produces the least amount of interference while optimizing signal strength.
- **Use of External Antennas**: If you wish to improve signal reception, consider utilizing an external antenna. When it comes to signal collection, exterior antennas are frequently more effective than inside antennas, and they can be strategically placed to avoid interference.
- **Power Supply Quality**: Ensure that your GMRS radio's power supply is both dependable and clean. Poor-quality power supplies can introduce electrical noise, causing interference. Always use high-quality power adapters and avoid sharing power with other electrical devices.

- **Interference Filters**: Some GMRS radios include built-in squelch or interference filters. Modifying these settings can help eliminate undesired signals and reduce background noise.
- **Avoiding Electronic Devices**: Keep GMRS radios away from other electronic devices that might cause radioactive interference. This category includes devices like Wi-Fi routers, cordless phones, and other related communication equipment.
- **Terrain and Obstruction Considerations**: You should be aware of the geography and physical impediments in your region. Obstacles such as mountains, buildings, and dense foliage can all reduce signal strength and cause interference. It may be necessary to change your location or the orientation of your antenna.
- **Time of Operation**: Some interference sources may be more active at different times of the day. To limit the harmful impacts of interference, you should, if possible, modify your communication schedule.
- **External Interference Sources**: Identify and address any sources of external interference in your local vicinity. The issue might originate from electrical power lines, industrial machinery, or other radio transmitters. Reduce your exposure to these sources as much as possible, or use shielding if you can.
- **Regular Maintenance**: Check that your GMRS radio and all of its components are in working condition. It is critical to check for potential sources of interference, such as loose connections, damaged cables, or worn-out components. Maintenance conducted on a regular basis ensures maximum performance.

It is vital to remember that the specific interference challenges you have may vary depending on your location and surroundings. You will be able to build effective mitigation strategies for RF interference in GMRS communication if you experiment with a number of techniques and become aware of the unique circumstances that exist in your operating environment.

Easy Way to Tune a GMRS Antenna

It is possible that you will need to tweak your antenna or "set the SWR" before using a GMRS radio installed in your overland vehicle. This is required to achieve the greatest outcomes. When we drive off-road with our pals, we enjoy utilizing these adaptive radios. However, for them to perform properly, you will most likely need to give them a little tune-up before using them. This will guarantee that you receive the best possible performance from them.

What is the relevance of calibrating your GMRS radio so that it works with your antenna. If you don't, any mismatch that occurs as a result of having the improper antenna length may degrade the performance of your radio or, worse, cause it to fail.

GMRS Antenna Basics: What Is SWR?

SWR is an acronym for "standing wave ratio," which is a measurement of how much radio frequency (RF) power is reflected back into your radio from the antenna rather than going in the desired direction, which is outward. Any radio frequency (RF) that is reflected back into your GMRS radio dramatically reduces the power of the signal you are sending, and it may cause damage to your radio's final amplifier.

Using the chart presented below, you can determine how much power is lost at each SWR level.

SWR Reading	% OF LOSS	ERP*	Power Output in Watts	Power Loss in Watts
1.0:1	0.0%	100.0%	100.00	0.0
1.1:1	0.2%	99.8%	99.8	0.2
1.2:1	0.8%	99.2%	99.2	0.8
1.3:1	1.7%	98.3%	98.3	1.7
1.4:1	2.8%	97.2%	97.2	2.8
1.5:1	4.0%	96.0%	96	4.0
1.6:1	5.3%	94.7%	94.7	5.3
1.7:1	6.7%	93.3%	93.3	6.7
1.8:1	8.2%	91.8%	91.8	8.2
2.0:1	11.1%	88.9%	88.9	11.1
2.2:1	14.1%	85.9%	85.9	14.1
2.4:1	17.0%	83.0%	83	17.0
2.6:1	19.8%	80.2%	80.2	19.8
3.0:1	25.0%	75.0%	75	25
4.0:1	36.0%	64.0%	64	36
5.0:1	44.4%	55.6%	55.6	44.4
6.0:1	51.0%	49.0%	49	51
7.0:1	56.3%	43.8%	43.8	56.3
8.0:1	60.5%	39.5%	39.5	60.5
9.0:1	64.0%	36.0%	36	64
10.0:1	66.9%	33.1%	33.1	66.9

Easiest Way to Set GMRS Radio SWR

You will need the following tools to modify the SWR on your GMRS radio:

- The SWR meter is a gadget. Examples of "no set" models that do not require tuning are the Fumei RS-40* and the Surecom SW-102. These are our favorite models. The Fumei RS-40 includes connectors that are common to most GMRS mobiles. Please be aware that a CB SWR meter will not work correctly on your GMRS radio because it is meant for a different frequency range.
- Small Allen wrench.
- Bolt cutters.
- A UHF Male Pl-259 to UHF Male Pl-259 jumper cable. (This links the meter with the radio.)

Step 1. Of Setting GMRS Radio SWR

- Move your automobile outdoors, away from barriers.
- To listen to GMRS, set your radio to channel 16.
- Set the transmission power to "**low**".
- To connect the meter, place your radio's antenna on the "ANT" side and connect the "**TX**" side using a jumper. The "range" switch should be set to the correct wattage.
- Ensure the channel is clear before giving your call sign and "testing." Then, key your microphone and check the meter reading. If it is 1.5/1 or less, you are good to go at that point. You will need to go to step 2 of the procedure if it is higher.
- Take accurate readings before proceeding.

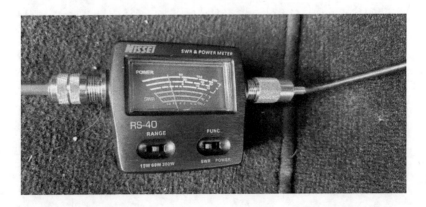

Step 2. Of Setting GMRS Radio SWR

- Use a black marker to mark the location within the base where the antenna will fit as a reference for future processes.
- Start by removing the screws that keep the antenna in place. After that, pull it as high as you can while still being able to tighten the screws. This will allow you to increase the length of the antenna.
- Return to your radio, hit the microphone button, and take note of the reading. If the SWR has suddenly risen, your antenna has to be shorter.
- Tighten the screws if the reading is less than 2.0/1. Consider the condition satisfactory. (If this is the case, you may want an antenna that can be extended farther.)
- If the reading is greater than expected, reposition the antenna below the black point you set. Recheck the SWR. If it is down, you're going in the right way. Let's call it great if it's less than 1.5/1.
- Your antenna length will need to be reduced if your SWR is still more than 1.5/1. Proceed to the third step.

Step 3: Cutting Your Stainless-Steel Antenna

- Use a vise to clamp the antenna length down. Although you can get by without a vise, having one is really useful.
- Use bolt cutters to cut off no more than half a centimeter (13/4 inch).
- Tighten the screws and insert the antenna into the base as far as it will go to evaluate the signal-to-noise ratio (SWR) once more. When the reading is less than 1/5:1, you can proceed. If that is not the case, you may need to repeat the method a few times.

It is vital to note that after you have shortened your antenna, you cannot reverse the operation. Before initiating any cutting activities, ensure that you are "moving in the right direction" with respect to the SWR. Even while the lowest SWR possible is certainly the ideal, you shouldn't be too concerned because an SWR less than 1.5/1 will not result in a significant improvement in performance.

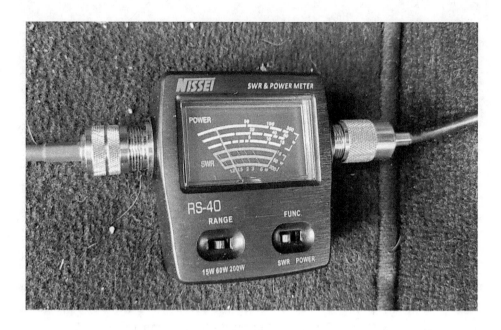

Increase GMRS Radio Power and Range

GMRS Radio Linear Amplifier

GMRS radio is quickly becoming the primary mode of communication in the off-road and overland groups. Because of the rapid adoption of these portable radios, as well as the availability of low-cost imported hardware, the bulk of which is not approved by the FCC, there appears to be substantial doubt about what is permissible on GMRS, such as linear power amplifiers. If the highest permissible GMRS output is fifty watts, couldn't you install a fifty-watt linear amplifier in your fifteen-watt Midland Micromobile to improve its transmission range?

However, despite being illegal, linear amplifiers have long been popular among CB users. These amplifiers can boost RF strength while producing very little distortion. Ham radio operators may legitimately use linear amplifiers, with certain bands permitting up to 1,500 watts of power. However, General Mobile Radio Service (GMRS) subscribers do not have the same privileges.

Can You Use a Linear Amplifier for GMRS Radio?

Unfortunately, the answer is no; a linear amplifier cannot be utilized with any GMRS radio under any circumstances. This is because all equipment used on GMRS channels must meet FCC part 95 standards. There is no GMRS linear amplifier on the market that is legal and recognized by Part 95.

These devices may be "**part 90 accepted**," but not "**part 95 accepted**," which the Federal Communications Commission considers inadequate. Not only do amplifiers like the BTech ones available online lack any circuitry that would restrict power on channels 1-7 (where only 5 watts are authorized), but there is also a power limitation on those channels.

Even though the Baofeng UV-5R portable devices may be purchased online and operate on GMRS channels, using them on GMRS signals is still forbidden. This applies even when the equipment is available for purchase online. The Federal Communications Commission (FCC) has imposed penalties of more than $10,000 for the use of linear amplifiers, despite the fact that the rule is infrequently enforced.

How To Legally Boost GMRS Radio Power

Fortunately, there are a few legal methods for increasing the output of GMRS radios that will not result in an expensive fine from the Federal Communications Commission.

Setting the GMRS Radio SWR

The power reflected back into your radio as a result of a mismatched antenna is significantly less than the power that might be broadcast in the desired direction. Therefore, establishing the GMRS Radio SWR is critical. A high SWR of 2.0:1 would result in approximately 5.5 watts of power loss, and worse, it might destroy your radio. This is an example based on a 50-watt output.

Power Isn't Everything

When using GMRS radios, remember that having a "line of sight" between you and another radio is more important than increasing the power of the radio. When there are impediments in the way, or when the other radio is below the "radio horizon," which is just slightly longer than the true line of sight, increasing the power will not result in much of an improvement.

Proper Antenna Placement for GMRS Radio Antennas

A GMRS radio antenna should be positioned in the center of your car's roof since this is the best location. This is due to the fact that the "ground plane" created by your car's metal roof creates the most unilateral distribution of radiated power, as well as the fact that the higher you set your antenna, the better it will operate. When it comes to off-road use, this may not always be the best option, especially if there are branches dangling over the side.

It is usual practice for Australian overlanders to mount their high-frequency (HF) outback radio antennas on the front of their cars, on the massive grill guards that also serve as a great ground plane. Regarding our overland setup, we initially attempted to put it on the side of our vehicle's bed rack, which proved to be less than successful. After considerable thought, we chose to install an NMO mount in the center of the cab of our car. This installation worked considerably better using our 5/8 wave GMRS antenna.

The following example shows how power is radiated from different antenna placements on an automobile.

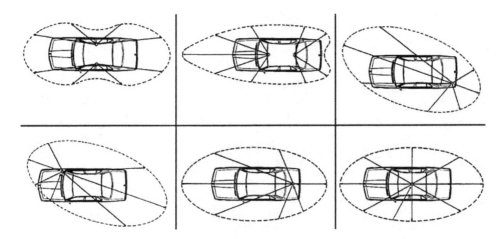

Replacing Your Stock Mobile or Handheld GMRS Antenna With a High Gain Model

Increasing the ERP, or effective radiated power, by upgrading to a high-gain GMRS antenna is one of the most efficient and legal ways to increase the amount of radio power generated from GMRS frequencies. When it comes to our transportable setup, we chose the Tram Browning BR-180-B, which is a dual-band antenna designed for both VHF and UHF ham radio frequencies. Because GMRS resides in the UHF region, it is an excellent fit for this application, providing a gain of 5.5 dB on GMRS channels. When we go along pathways with a lot of branches hanging over the road, we can quickly unscrew the NMO mount and replace it with a Midland ghost antenna.

In addition to being an excellent choice for off-road vehicles, the Midland MXTA-26, a non-motorized mount, is what we use on our old Jeep. It is a single-band GMRS antenna with a more streamlined look thanks to the elimination of the second loading coil seen in the ANLI WH-713. It also features an impressive 6 dB gain.

If you accidentally brush against some of the above-mentioned limbs, the MXTA-26 is protected by a solid spring basis. In addition to being compatible with Midland magnetic and L-bracket installations, you can drill a hole in your cab's roof and execute a flush mount if you want a more visually acceptable installation and are willing to invest.

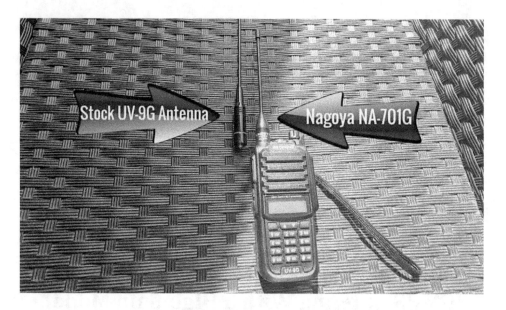

Other Ways to Increase GMRS Radio Range

Utilize the high-power GMRS channels 15-22, which allow you to use 50 watts of electricity if you have a full-power mobile device. This will allow you to have a larger range. Your gadget should have a high/low power mode, which you can set to high to enhance the amount of power generated. Aim to use as little power as possible for day-to-day use, and if you can, consider using one of the 5-watt channels, which run from 1-7, to avoid the congestion that occurs on channels 15-22, which are often utilized.

If you want to make a call from your mobile phone or portable device, try to wait until you're out in the open and free of any nearby impediments. If feasible, attempt to make the call from a higher vantage point. The radio frequency (RF) from your smartphone will not be absorbed by the objects in close proximity.

GMRS Repeaters

If you have a GMRS radio that can repeat sound, you can use it to access repeater stations throughout the United States. When they are linked to the internet, they act as a relay station, which means they may re-broadcast your signal across a much broader area, and in some cases, the entire country. Despite the fact that some of them are private and inaccessible to the general public, the vast majority of them are open to the public and may be utilized courteously.

Two Examples of GMRS Radio Range

A real-world GMRS radio range is illustrated below, including the distance from base to mobile, mobile to mobile, and mobile to portable. There are other options available, and the results may change significantly from those illustrated here.

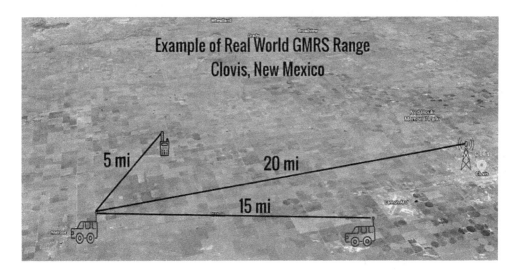

The second image (shown below) was created using Radio Mobile, an internet radio range calculator particularly developed for amateur radio operators. Using GMRS radio, it displays the possible range that may be obtained from the summit of Pikes summit, which stands at 14,115 inches.

We added this to highlight how range is a very subjective idea that is primarily governed by the elevation of your antenna. The output power and height of the receiving antenna are the next most essential considerations.

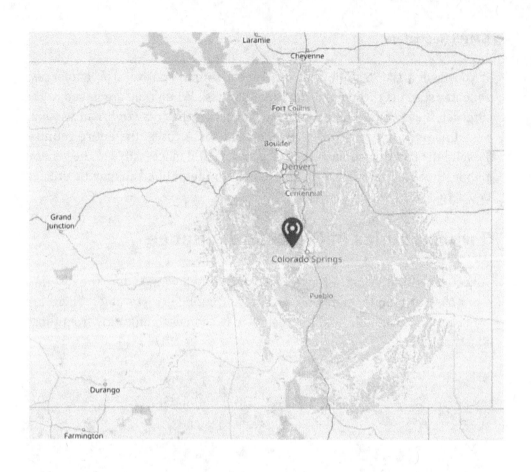

Chapter 4

Operating Your GMRS Radio

Overview of Key Features and Buttons

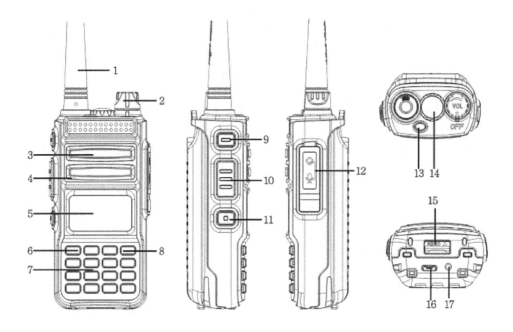

1. **Antenna**: Used to enhance the radio's signal reception and transmission.
2. **Power/Volume Control**: Rotate to turn the radio on or off and adjust the volume.
3. **Speaker**: Outputs sound for communication or alerts.
4. **Microphone**: Allows you to speak during transmission.
5. **LCD Display**: Shows important information such as frequency, battery status, and settings.
6. **(MENU) Key**: Access the menu functions and confirm your selections. In standby mode, press and hold to toggle between frequency mode and channel mode.
7. **Alphanumeric Keypad**: Used for entering numbers or selecting options from the menu.

8. ⊃/🔊 **(Back/WX) Key**: Press to exit the menu or other functions. Press and hold for 5 seconds to switch between GMRS communication mode and NOAA weather reception mode.
9. **FM/SOS Key**: Press briefly to activate the FM radio. Press again to turn it off. Hold to activate the audible and visual SOS alarm.
10. **PTT Key**: Push-to-talk key for transmitting your voice. Hold to speak and release to listen for incoming calls.
11. **LAMP/Monitor Key**: Press once to turn on the flashlight, press and hold to activate a flashing mode, and press again to turn it off. Also holds to activate MONITOR mode.
12. **MIC/SP Jacks**: Connects to an external speaker or microphone.
13. **LED Indicators**: Red LED indicates transmission, green LED indicates reception.
14. **Flashlight**: Provides light when needed, activated by the LAMP key.
15. **Battery Release Latch**: Unlocks the battery compartment for battery replacement.
16. **Type-C Charging Port**: For charging the radio using a DC 5V USB input.
17. **Charging Indicator**: Red light indicates charging, green light indicates a full charge.

Main Controls and Parts of the Radio

LCD Display

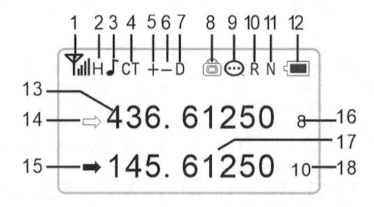

1. **Received Signal Strength**: Indicates the strength of the received signal.
2. **Power Selection (High/Low)**: Displays whether the radio is set to high or low power for transmission.
3. **DTMFST Activation**: Appears when DTMF (Dual-Tone Multi-Frequency Signaling) or ANI (Automatic Number Identification) is activated.
4. **DCS/CTCSS Code**: These symbols show when a DCS or CTCSS privacy code is set for transmitting (TX) or receiving (RX). In TX mode, it appears when you're transmitting, and in RX mode, it shows up even in standby mode.
5. **Positive Shift Activated**: Appears when a positive frequency shift is enabled.
6. **Negative Shift Activated**: Appears when a negative frequency shift is enabled.
7. **Dual Watch Function**: Displays when the Dual Watch feature is active, allowing monitoring of two channels simultaneously.
8. **Keypad Lock**: This icon shows that the keypad is locked. To unlock it, press [ ].
9. **VOX Function Enabled**: Indicates that the Voice-Activated Transmission (VOX) function is turned on.
10. **Reverse Frequency**: Indicates when the radio is set to reverse frequency mode.
11. **Narrow Bandwidth (N)**: "N" indicates narrow bandwidth mode. If the radio is in wide bandwidth (W) mode, no icon is displayed.
12. **Battery Level Indicator**: Shows the current battery level. If the battery is almost depleted, the icon will blink, and transmission will be blocked until the radio is charged.
13. 13/17. **Frequency/Channel Display**: Depending on the setting, this icon shows the current frequency, channel name, or menu setting.
14. 14/15. **VFO/Menu/Function Indicator**: Shows which Variable Frequency Oscillator (VFO) is in use and the current menu or function setting. This icon appears near the frequency band or menu settings.
15. 16/18. **Stored Channel Number**: Displays the channel number you have stored in memory.

How to Make and Receive Calls

1. **Turn on the Radio**:
   - First, ensure that your GMRS radio is powered on by rotating the power/volume control to the "on" position. Adjust the volume to a level where you can hear incoming transmissions clearly.
2. **Select the Right Channel**:
   - Use the **channel selector** to choose the channel you want to use. Make sure both parties are tuned into the same channel so that you can communicate.
3. **Prepare to Transmit**:
   - To make a call, press and hold the **PTT (Push-to-Talk)** key. This key activates the transmission, allowing you to speak into the radio's microphone.
4. **Speak Clearly**:
   - While holding down the PTT key, speak clearly into the microphone. Make sure to speak at a moderate pace and volume to ensure your message is understood.
5. **Release the PTT Key**:
   - Once you've finished speaking, release the PTT key. This will switch the radio back to receive mode, allowing the other party to respond.
6. **Wait for a Response**:
   - After releasing the PTT key, listen for a reply. If the other party wants to respond, they will press their PTT key to transmit it back to you.

How to Receive a Call

1. **Listen for Incoming Calls**:
   - When the radio is in **receive mode** (i.e., after you've released the PTT key or when the radio is idle), you will hear any incoming calls or messages from others on the same channel.
2. **Adjust the Volume**:
   - If the volume is too low or too high, adjust the **volume control** until the incoming message is at a comfortable level.
   -

3. **Respond**:
    o   If you receive a message and wish to respond, simply press and hold the **PTT key** to speak back to the other party.
    o   Make sure to wait for the other person to release their PTT key before speaking, as both parties cannot transmit simultaneously on the same channel.

Channels, Privacy Codes, and Their Uses

Channels and privacy codes are critical components of GMRS radios, enabling efficient and confidential communication. Understanding how these components function together can help you get the most out of your GMRS radio, especially while communicating in a busy or noisy setting.

Channels

GMRS radios use a set of predefined channels within particular frequency bands. To transmit and receive signals between radios, these channels are utilized. The GMRS frequency range is 462 MHz to 467 MHz, with each channel corresponding to a distinct frequency within that range. GMRS radios normally have 22 channels, although some may have more, particularly if they offer repeater access.

Each channel on a GMRS radio represents a specific frequency that allows communication between radios tuned to the same channel. Channels 1–7 are shared with FRS (Family Radio Service) radios, whereas channels 8–14 are reserved solely for GMRS usage. Channels 15-22 are shared by both FRS and GMRS radios, although GMRS radios may transmit at higher strength, which is one of the main distinctions between GMRS and FRS radios.

When you pick a channel on your GMRS radio, you are effectively tuning it to a certain frequency. The radio will only receive signals from other radios on the same frequency, so be sure that all radios in your communication are tuned to the same channel. This enables clear and consistent communication, whether you're utilizing GMRS radios for outdoor activities, family conversation, or emergency situations.

Some GMRS radios provide access to repeater channels. These channels are used in combination with a repeater, which is a device that receives a weak signal and retransmits it with increased power. Repeaters increase the range of your transmission, which is especially effective in obstructive terrain like mountains or deep forests. Repeaters allow users to communicate over far greater distances than a portable GMRS radio alone.

Privacy Codes

Channels determine the frequency a GMRS radio is tuned to, whereas privacy codes (also known as CTCSS or DCS codes) decrease interference and promote privacy by screening out undesirable communications on the channel. These codes effectively provide a layer of privacy to your connection by allowing you to hear only communications from radios broadcasting on the same channel and privacy code.

Privacy codes are not encryption techniques, thus they do not fully safeguard your connection. Instead, they function more as a filter. When a radio is set to a certain channel with a privacy code, it will only transmit or receive signals from other radios on that channel with the same code. If another user on the same channel does not utilize the same privacy code, your radio will not receive their communications. This can assist in avoiding interruptions from unrelated discussions or interference from radios using the same channel.

GMRS radios frequently employ two types of privacy codes: CTCSS (Continuous Tone-Coded Squelch System) and DCS.

- **CTCSS**: This is the most prevalent privacy code for GMRS radios. It sends analog sub-audible tones together with the broadcast. These tones allow the receiving radio to filter out signals from other radios that do not use the same tone. There are normally 38 CTCSS tones available for usage, and you can select which one to use for each channel.
- **DCS**: This offers a digital alternative to CTCSS. It achieves the same effect by employing digital codes rather than analog tones. There are 83 DCS codes available, which give more alternatives than CTCSS codes. Some radios may let users utilize either CTCSS or DCS codes, depending on their preferences.

By employing privacy codes, you can keep your talks reasonably secret, even if others are using the same channel. However, it is crucial to remember that privacy codes do not prevent others from hearing your conversation if they are on the same channel and use a matching privacy code. Essentially, privacy codes limit unwanted interference but do not give complete protection.

How Channels and Privacy Codes Work Together

Channels and privacy rules collaborate to provide transparent, private, and coordinated communication. When you choose a channel, you are selecting a certain frequency for communication. If you want to ensure that no one else can listen in on your talk, you can pick a privacy code beside the channel.

For example, if you're on Channel 5 and have the CTCSS tone set to 14, you'll only be able to hear communication from other Channel 5 users who have the same tone. This allows you to avoid hearing irrelevant broadcasts from other users who may be on the same channel but use different privacy codes. This is especially handy when numerous organizations are utilizing the same channel for various reasons. For example, during a family camping vacation, each group might use a unique privacy code on the same channel to keep their chats private and avoid overlap.

One of the primary benefits of employing privacy codes is that they reduce cross-talk and interference. This can be especially crucial when you're in crowded settings like parks or campers, where numerous users may be using the same channels simultaneously. Without privacy codes, everyone on the same channel would hear each other's discussions, perhaps causing misunderstanding or unwelcome interruptions.

Practical Applications of Channels and Privacy Codes

- GMRS radios are commonly used in outdoor activities such as hiking, camping, off-roading, and skiing. When participating in these activities as a group, employing specialized channels and privacy codes provides clear communication free of interruption from other groups in the region. You can eliminate crosstalk from unrelated parties by employing GMRS-specific channels and privacy codes.

- GMRS radios can serve as a lifeline in emergency situations if standard communication networks are unavailable. By choosing a suitable channel and privacy code, you can secure uninterrupted contact with your group. Furthermore, if there is a local repeater, utilizing repeater channels can greatly increase your communication range.

- GMRS radios are commonly used for family communication, particularly in big parks or outdoor activities. Using privacy codes allows each family to converse privately on the same channel, free of interference from others. This can be especially handy when many families are utilizing radios in the same region.

- GMRS radios can offer a dependable and convenient communication option for small enterprises, such as those working in big warehouses, construction sites, or security teams. Businesses can guarantee that their employees communicate successfully by adopting particular channels and privacy codes that prevent interference from the general public or other businesses using the same radio frequencies.

Communication Best Practices

1. Select the Right Channel and Privacy Code

Before commencing a conversation, ensure that you and the persons you're chatting with are on the same channel and using the same privacy code. This is critical for avoiding interference from other users and ensuring that your message is received correctly. Channels in GMRS radios are assigned to certain frequencies, thus ensuring that everyone is using the same channel. Furthermore, utilizing privacy codes (CTCSS or DCS) can aid in filtering out signals from others who may be using the same channel.

Best Practice: If you're in a group, decide on a channel and privacy code ahead of time to guarantee everyone can chat without interruptions.

2. Use Clear and Concise Language

When talking using GMRS radio, utilize precise and simple language to guarantee that your message is understood. Radios are not as clear as phone conversations, so speaking slowly and clearly can help prevent misinterpretation. Avoid using sophisticated vocabulary or jargon that others may not understand, especially if you're in a group situation with varying degrees of radio expertise.

Best Practice: Use short, straightforward phrases. Avoid superfluous words or lengthy explanations. This helps to keep the conversation flowing and prevents critical information from being lost.

3. Identify Yourself and Others

When making a call on the GMRS radio, begin by identifying yourself and the person or group you are attempting to interact with. This guarantees that everyone understands who is speaking and prevents misunderstanding when numerous individuals use the same channel.

For example, while contacting someone, you may say, **"This is John, calling Sarah on Channel 5. Do you copy?"** This approach is especially useful in a noisy or packed location when many people may be broadcasting at the same time.

Best Practice: Always identify yourself at the start of each call, and repeat the identity as necessary. This makes it easy for everyone to identify who is speaking.

4. Use the Push-to-Talk (PTT) Key Properly

The Push-to-Talk (PTT) key is the primary way to transmit your voice over the GMRS radio. It is critical to remember to hold down the PTT key while speaking and release it when you are finished so that the other person can react. If you keep the PTT button pushed after speaking, the other person may miss a portion of your message or not hear it at all.

Best Practice: Press the PTT key before speaking, and then release it when completed. Wait for the other person to talk before pushing the PTT key again.

5. Wait for the Other Person to Finish

Unlike phone calls, GMRS radios require users to take turns speaking. When one person transmits, the other cannot talk until the transmission is completed. This indicates that you should wait for the other person to complete speaking before pressing the PTT key to react. Interrupting or speaking over someone can result in missing information or misunderstanding.

Best Practice: Wait until the other person has finished speaking and released their PTT key before responding with your own. This promotes seamless, organized communication.

6. Minimize Background Noise

Background noise can disrupt the quality of your broadcast. If you're in a noisy location, consider moving to a quieter area or using an external microphone or headset with a jack on your GMRS radio. Also, avoid making excessive noises like screaming, loud breathing, or talking while moving, as they can distort your message and make it harder for the listener to comprehend you.

Best Practice: Whenever feasible, move to a quieter environment or use noise-reducing gear.

7. Keep It Short and to the Point

Radio communication does not allow for protracted pauses or back-and-forth exchanges as phone calls do. Because GMRS radios communicate in real-time, make your communications brief, clear, and to the point. This decreases the likelihood of someone missing essential information and promotes a rapid flow of communication.

Best Practice: Don't chat for too long. Try to deliver your message in short, basic words so that the recipient can easily grasp and reply.

8. Use Call Signs and Radio Etiquette

Using call signs (a unique name or identification for each radio user) can aid in distinguishing amongst speakers in group conversations, particularly with bigger teams or during emergency circumstances. Radio etiquette also involves being polite, respectful, and considerate of those who use the same frequency. Keep in mind that GMRS radios are a common resource, so please use them wisely.

Best Practice: Use call signs for each member of your group, and maintain good radio etiquette by being respectful and not monopolizing the channel.

9. Limit Radio Overuse

GMRS radios are a shared resource, therefore avoid hogging the frequency or speaking too much at once. If the channel is congested or others are waiting for their turn to talk, keep your communication brief and give others a chance to transmit. This is especially crucial when numerous users are in the same area or when the radio is being used in group settings.

Best Practice: Limit your radio use, especially in group situations, so that everyone gets a chance to speak. If the channel is congested, limit the amount of time you spend sending.

10. Monitor the Channel

If you're not actively chatting, you can put your radio into monitor mode to listen for incoming calls or crucial messages. Monitoring enables you to be aware of the communication around you, particularly in emergency situations, without actively participating in a conversation. Many GMRS radios have a monitor button or function that allows you to listen for weak signals or active communication on the channel.

Best Practice: Keep your radio in monitor mode when you're not actively talking, especially in group settings or emergencies, to stay up to date on communication.

11. Use Repeaters for Extended Range

Consider utilizing repeaters in regions where topography or distance may make communication difficult. Repeaters increase the range of your GMRS radio by amplifying and re-transmitting the signal over a broader region. If you're in a low-signal region or need to contact someone further away, connecting your radio to a repeater can significantly increase your communication range.

Best Practice: Use repeaters to increase your communication range as needed. Make sure you understand how to access repeaters and how they operate with your GMRS radio's settings.

12. Emergency Communication

When cell coverage is lacking, GMRS radios can be an invaluable tool for rapid communication in an emergency. When utilizing GMRS radios in emergency situations, remember that brevity and clarity are essential. Provide critical information, such as your location, the nature of the incident, and any particular requests for assistance. Emergency communication should be precise, succinct, and focused on receiving the right support.

Best Practice: In an emergency, deliver critical information swiftly and without superfluous conversation. Focus on obtaining assistance or delivering critical information.

GMRS Radio Etiquette

1. Identify Yourself Clearly

Before transmitting, always identify yourself so that the individual or group with whom you are interacting knows who is speaking. This is especially critical in group settings or when starting a call. Simply saying your name or call sign can serve as identification. This method clarifies who is speaking, avoids uncertainty, and enables people to respond properly.

Example: "This is John phoning Sarah. Do you copy? "

When responding to someone, use their call sign or name to indicate that you are addressing them directly. This provides clarity and reduces misunderstanding when numerous users use the same channel.

2. Keep Your Messages Short and Clear

One of the most important tenets of GMRS radio etiquette is to make your communications brief. Radios have limited bandwidth and can only handle brief bursts of communication. When speaking on the radio, avoid extended phrases and superfluous information. Get to the point quickly, especially in time-sensitive circumstances.

Instead of saying, "Hey, I was thinking we could maybe meet up at the trailhead and then figure out what to do next," say, "Sarah, this is John." Are you at the trailhead? "

Short, straightforward communications lessen the likelihood of someone losing vital information or having problems comprehending your message.

3. Wait for a Response

Always wait for the other person to complete speaking before pressing the Push-to-Talk (PTT) button. This is especially significant when numerous people use the same channel. Interrupting or talking over someone can result in lost communication and misunderstanding. If you're on a shared channel with others, respect the channel time and let the other person complete speaking before answering.

4. Be Polite and Courteous

Good manners are important in all forms of communication. Radio etiquette stresses courtesy, especially while communicating in a group or on a channel with others. Avoid screaming, cursing, and using unpleasant words. Others can pick up radio messages, and being nasty or inconsiderate can cause the entire communication system to fail.

Best Practice: Signal that you have completed speaking and are waiting for a response by using phrases like "Please," "Thank you," and "Over."

Example: "John, this is Sarah. Please confirm if you've reached the campsite. Over."

5. Use the Correct Channel

Always verify that you are communicating through the right channel. GMRS radios have numerous channels, so make sure everyone in your group is on the same one. Before sending, ensure that the channel is clear and that others on the same channel are not engaged in other discussions.

6. Limit Radio Usage

Although GMRS radios are useful for staying in touch, it is critical to avoid monopolizing the channel. If numerous persons are utilizing the same frequency, giving others time to talk and not overusing the radio improves communication and guarantees that everyone has a chance to be heard.

7. Use Call Signs

When working in a group or with several users, employing call signals can assist you in determining who is speaking. This is especially beneficial in emergency situations or when several individuals are chatting simultaneously. A call sign is a unique identification that helps to avoid misunderstanding and guarantees that everyone can follow the discussion.

If you're working with a family or group, each member can be given a unique name or identify for simple identification. In a more formal or professional context, you may be required to utilize certain call signs given by your business or team.

8. Avoid Overusing the Radio

Because GMRS radios are a shared resource, it's critical to limit how frequently you transmit. Avoid utilizing the radio for non-essential communication, especially if there are few channels available. If you're communicating in a busy location or during an emergency, limit the amount of time you spend sending to prevent interfering with other important messages.

9. Use the Proper Tone and Volume

Because GMRS radios frequently have poor sound quality, it's critical to talk at a reasonable level and in a clear, controlled tone. Yelling or speaking too quietly can make it difficult for the receiver to hear or comprehend you, particularly in a noisy or windy area.

10. Respect Other Users on the Same Channel

GMRS radio channels are shared, which means that several users may be utilizing the same channel at the same time. If you find the channel is busy or in use, don't transmit until it's clear. Being respectful of other users helps to prevent disrupting their talks and ensures that everyone can interact efficiently.

CHAPTER 5

GMRS RADIO SETTINGS AND CONFIGURATION

Adjusting Squelch and Volume Levels

People who use cordless walkie-talkies may suffer unpleasant sounds when sleeping due to internal noise. When internal noise produces a loud "rustle" sound at the audio output end, especially when there is no received signal, it can be irritating and cause confusion and listening fatigue.

To address this issue, two-way radios with wireless contact include a squelch circuit. This circuit is critical for improving the user experience since it automatically reduces or mutes low-level noise when the device is not in use or there is no signal coming in.

When the radio is in sleep mode or no calls are received, the squelch circuit locks the low-frequency amplifier. It effectively prevents unwanted noise from reaching the speaker or headphones by doing this. You can tell when a received signal is detected because the squelch circuit alters on the fly to let the signal pass while blocking low-level noise.

This delay function not only improves music quality by eliminating distracting noise but also makes listening more pleasant and less taxing for consumers. It ensures that the communication connection remains clear and free of interference during calm periods, making walkie-talkies a more efficient and helpful method to communicate while on the road.

In two-way radio transmission, the quantity of background noise is proportional to the intensity of the signal being heard, as you said. People frequently find themselves in circumstances where a strong signal means little to no noise and a weak signal means a lot of noise, making it difficult to grasp what is being said.

Due to these issues, the mute button on a two-way radio is an essential tool for consumers. The silent function is intended to maintain a balance between valuable signals and background noise by automatically shutting off or muting low-level noise when no signals are delivered.

The silent function must be properly configured for optimal transmission quality in a variety of scenarios. When the received signal is strong, users can increase the delay level by selecting a higher cutoff. This reduces low-level noise and maintains the audio output clean. When the signal is weaker, reduce the quiet level to hear weaker signals, even if they are intermingled with background noise.

This dynamic modification to the squelch function aids in achieving a healthy balance between noise suppression and allowing lower-level messages to be heard. It is especially essential when the distance between the two individuals communicating varies, as the intensity of the signal heard is proportional to how close the sender is.

To summarize, utilizing the silent function appropriately and customizing it to the discussion scenario is critical for achieving the optimal balance of relevant information and noise. This ensures that two-way radio communication is clear and effective in a range of conditions.

Squelch Switch

It's a function key designed to address the issue of radio calls being either quiet or too clear.

Tips on How to Set the Noise Level

We know that different radios have varying amounts of quiet. The level is modified based on the user's interaction needs and the environment in which they are.

- When communicating over a longer distance, the signal will weaken. This requires a decreased noise level and improved reception sensitivity.
- When communicating with a close user and receiving a strong signal, increase the squelch level or adjust the squelch depth. This will reduce noise.

- Interruptions during a call indicate a poor radio signal or that the signal can no longer be heard due to distance. At this stage, the noise level should be reduced to increase sensitivity.

In most circumstances, the level should be set higher if the distance between the two persons is short. It's farther out in the wild, thus the level should be reduced.

Because each model is classified differently, sometimes you can only go by what you know and use the original setting as a reference.

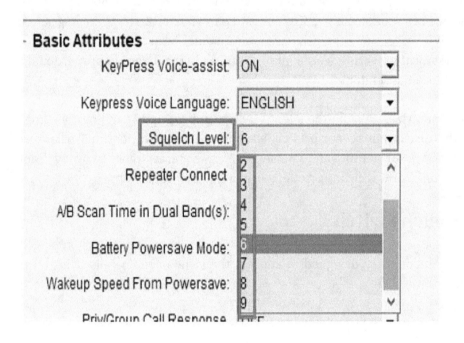

Channel Scanning Configuration

GMRS radios feature a valuable capability called "channel scanning" that allows users to listen to more than one channel for action. This helps them identify ongoing discussions or essential communications. Here's a thorough look at how GMRS radios are configured for channel scanning:

1. **Scan Types**: GMRS radios typically feature many scan kinds, such as

- **Priority Scan:** This scans through certain channels in a certain order, giving some channels more weight than others.
- **Dual Watch Scan:** Watches two channels back-to-back and quickly switches between them.
- **All Channels Scan:** Look through all channels to find the ones that are currently being used for communication.

2. **Manual vs. Auto Scan:**

- **Manual Scan:** With manual scanning, users choose which channels to scan and start the scanning process themselves.
- **Auto Scan:** The radio will instantly switch between stations based on settings that have already been set or user preferences.

3. **Scan Delay:** A scan delay lets users choose how long the radio stays on one station before switching to the next one. This function lets you record longer talks so you don't miss any of the action.
4. **Channel Skip:** During the search process, users may be able to skip over certain channels. This is helpful when the user knows that some stations are busy or don't matter and doesn't want to watch them.
5. **Scan Resume:** When a signal is found on a channel that is being searched, the scan may stop so that users can listen to the talk. The scan starts up again after the contact stops.
6. **Programmable Scan Lists:** Some GMRS radios let users make their scan lists that tell the radio which bands to scan and which to leave out. This helps make scans fit certain situations or wants.
7. **Priority Channels:** Users can make some channels more likely to be checked than others by marking them as priority channels. This is helpful when it's important to keep an eye on certain frequencies.
8. **Scan Confirmation Tones:** If the radio picks up the action while scanning, it may sound an alarm or play a tone. These tones let people know that a certain route is being used for conversation.
9. **Sub-Channels and Privacy Codes:** Scanning may also include listening to sub-channels or channels with certain privacy codes, depending on what the radio can do. This lets people find chats that have certain protection settings.
10. **Dual-Scanning Capability:** Some high-tech GMRS radios have dual-scanning features that let users listen to two sets of stations at the

same time. This helps people who need to keep up with a lot of different things.

11. **Programmable Buttons:** Radios with programmable buttons may let users add scanner tasks to certain buttons so they are easy to find and use.

12. **Scan Lockout:** Users may be able to quickly block or leave out certain channels from the scanning process. This helps when you want to avoid interruptions or messages that you don't want.

To enable channel scanning on a GMRS radio, navigate through the radio's menu system and select the scan settings you desire. The user handbook that comes with your GMRS radio has detailed instructions for configuring scanner settings. Understanding and utilizing the scanning functions can make GMRS radios more effective and efficient in a range of contact scenarios.

Radio System Integration and Interfacing

Radio System Integration and Interfacing with GMRS (General Mobile Radio Service) is the process of incorporating GMRS technology into a broader communication network to ensure that it operates seamlessly and efficiently. This approach requires a thorough understanding of both GMRS standards and the complete transmission system. When integrating GMRS into a larger radio system, there are a few key considerations:

- **Frequency Coordination:** Coordinating GMRS frequencies is crucial for effective communication. Radio systems typically operate within a certain frequency band. To function with the present system, GMRS' frequencies must be matched with its own to reduce crosstalk and maximize range.
- **Compatibility and Standards:** Ensure GMRS equipment satisfies all relevant specifications. To merge successfully, new radio tools, protocols, and transmission standards must be compatible with those that are already in use. Following the guidelines established by the Federal Communications Commission (FCC) ensures that activities are lawful and efficient.
- **Interoperability**: This is crucial for integrating radio systems and ensuring seamless communication. To do this, protocols, interfaces, and communication standards must be established so that GMRS

devices can communicate with other components of the system correctly.

- **Antenna and Transmission Line Considerations**: In order to implement GMRS, antennas, and communication lines may need to be examined and maybe modified so that they can accommodate the frequency range and power levels that GMRS uses. It is critical to ensure that signals are accurately transmitted and received for the entire system to function properly.

- **Optimized Power and Range**: GMRS utilizes more power than FRS, resulting in longer transmission ranges. To install GMRS, ensure that the power settings and range are tuned to align with the communication system's overall goals. To do this, broadcast power levels may need to be adjusted and repeaters used strategically.

- **System Validation and Testing**: It's crucial to properly test the merged system so that any issues that arise throughout the merging process can be identified and resolved. This involves testing signal clarity and performance, as well as ensuring that the built-in GMRS components meet or exceed the standards.

- **Security and Privacy**: Implementing appropriate security measures is crucial to ensure safe interactions inside the integrated system. To ensure the security of private data transmitted across the GMRS-integrated network, encryption and identification may be required.

- **Documentation and Training:** Detailed documentation and training are essential for the integrated system, including setup settings, working procedures, and problem-solving recommendations. The unified GMRS system runs smoothly and effectively because users and administrators are trained on its unique features and peculiarities.

To demonstrate how GMRS works, below is a fictitious scenario of adding it to a shipping company's existing radio communication system. In this instance, the firm operates a fleet of vehicles and employs a two-way radio system so that drivers, dispatchers, and supply managers can communicate quickly and conveniently.

Scenario: Logistics Company Integration of GMRS

- **Assessment of Current System**: The shipping firm now employs a VHF two-way radio on exclusive business bands. Before implementing GMRS, the present system is evaluated to see how it is used in terms of regularity, coverage, and communication requirements.

- **Frequency Coordination**: The company selects open GMRS bands that align with their operational needs while adhering to FCC regulations. Coordination is done to ensure that bands currently in use by the VHF system do not cause excessive confusion.

- **Equipment Selection and Standards Compliance**: FCC regulations and legislation are followed while selecting mobile radios and tiny devices for GMRS use. The chosen technology supports the appropriate radio bands and power levels for GMRS.

- **Interoperability Planning**: New GMRS devices can communicate with the existing VHF system using established protocols and interfaces. Compatibility testing ensures that both systems can communicate correctly with one another.

- **Antenna and Transmission Line Adjustments**: The GMRS frequency range is adjusted by altering antennas on automobiles and central dispatch. Taking into mind the greater power levels associated with GMRS, transmission lines are altered to ensure that signals flow as swiftly as feasible.

- **Power and Range Optimization:** Optimized power and range levels for GMRS radios based on shipping company contact requirements. Repeaters can be strategically placed to boost coverage and avoid signal difficulties in distant locations.

- **Testing and Validation**: The combo undergoes extensive testing to ensure functionality. This involves testing the signal's range and quality, as well as replicating real-world scenarios to identify and resolve any performance issues.

- **Security Implementation:** Encryption technologies on GMRS radios protect confidential corporate data. There are access controls and identification mechanisms in place to ensure that only those who are authorized can use the unified communication system.

- **Documentation and Training**: Develop a comprehensive collection of literature outlining the merging process, setup settings, and problem-solving methods. Drivers, dispatchers, and IT personnel all receive training to become used to the new GMRS capabilities and ensure that everything operates properly.

- **Deployment and Monitoring**: The system is implemented gradually and monitored for any issues. The integrated GMRS system will be subjected to frequent adjustments and repairs to ensure that it functions well.

CHAPTER 6
GMRS RADIO PROGRAMMING

Introduction to GMRS Radio Programming

Setting the right frequencies, squelch levels, and other settings like protection codes and power levels on a GMRS radio is part of programming it so that it works at its best. Selecting the proper frequencies to transmit and receive is the first step in programming a GMRS radio. Depending on the type of radio, you may need to enter the frequencies by hand or use software for programming. You can change settings on a lot of GMRS radios, like the power output, the silence levels (which lower background noise), and the privacy codes (also called CTCSS or DCS codes), which stop unwanted broadcasts.

As GMRS radios are frequently used with FRS (Family Radio Service) and other radio systems, some of which use channels that overlap, it's important to understand and set the correct channel for contact in addition to frequency settings. A lot of GMRS radios also have weather reports and scanning tools that can be useful for keeping an eye on other users or the conditions in your area.

It's also important to know that in the United States, you need a license to use a GMRS radio. The Federal Communications Commission (FCC) makes it easy to get the license, which lets the holder use GMRS devices on allowed frequencies. To keep things legal and to avoid interfering with other conversations, it's important to follow the rules and laws for using GMRS.

Basic Radio Programming Tools

You'll need certain apps and tools to set GMRS radios correctly. These tools help set up the radio's settings, such as its protection codes, frequencies, and power output. For GMRS radio programming, these are the basic radio programming tools and apps you'll need:

1. Programming Cable

Your GMRS radio and computer are linked by a programming wire. It lets frequency and setting information be sent from the radio to the computer. Depending on the model of the radio, the type of wire you need may vary. For older models, straight USB cables or USB-to-serial adapters are popular choices.

2. Radio Programming Software

- **CHIRP**: The CHIRP program is one of the most well-known and widely used free GMRS radio programming services. It works with many radios, including GMRS, and lets users enter frequencies, set up channels, change power settings, and set up protection codes. CHIRP can be used on Windows, macOS, and Linux. Its simple design makes it great for both new and experienced users.
- **Manufacturer-Specific Software**: Many GMRS radio brands provide their own proprietary programming software. For example:
    - **Baofeng (UV-5R, UV-82)** radios often use software like **Baofeng UV-5R software** or **CHIRP** for programming.
    - **Kenwood** and **Motorola** radios may use specialized software like **Kenwood MCP** or **Motorola CPS** (Customer Programming Software).
- This software typically comes with the radio or can be downloaded from the manufacturer's website.

3. Driver Software

Depending on the type of programming line you have, you might need to add more drivers to your computer so it can see the radio. You can usually get these drivers from the manufacturer's website or the company that makes the programming cord.

4. FCC Licensing Software (if required)

In the United States, you need a license to use a GMRS radio. The FCC has an online method called the FCC Universal Licensing method (ULS) that can be used to apply for this license. This is not directly linked to programming the radio, but it is needed to legally use the radio.

5. Firmware Updates (Optional)

For some radios to work at their best, the software may need to be updated, especially when new features or bug changes come out. Most of the time, you can make these changes by using the software that came with the radio or following the steps that came with it.

Step-by-Step Guide to Programming GMRS Radios

You need to set up both the radio and your other gear before you start programming your GMRS radio. This makes sure that your computer and radio can talk to each other without any problems and stops any programming problems.

1. Gather Your Equipment

- Make sure your GMRS batteries are fully charged or brand new, as programming may take a while.
- **Programming Cable**: Make sure you have the right wire to connect your radio to your computer. Depending on the type of radio you have, this could be a USB-to-serial cable or a straight USB wire.
- **Computer**: Make sure your computer has USB ports and is running the right operating system, such as Windows, macOS, or Linux.
- **Programming Software**: Get the software you need (like CHIRP or software made by the maker) and put it on your computer.
- **Drivers**: If the programming cord needs drivers, install them so the computer and radio can talk to each other.

2. Install the Programming Software

- If you use CHIRP or another third-party program like it, get it from the main page and put it on your computer.
- If you're using software made by the radio maker, like Motorola CPS or Baofeng UV-5R software, install it by following the directions that came with it or by downloading it from the maker's website.

3. Install Drivers for the Programming Cable (if necessary)

- Sometimes, your computer may need drivers for your programming cord to be able to see the device. Most of the time, you can find these drivers on the website of the wire maker or in the programming kit.
- If these cords don't already have a driver, you might need to install one like the Prolific PL2303 driver.

4. Connect the Radio to the Computer

- The programming cord needs to be plugged into both the radio and a USB port on your computer.
- Make sure that both the radio and the computer are safely linked to the wire.

5. Turn On the GMRS Radio

- Turn the knob or press the power button, based on your type, to turn on the radio.
- Make sure the radio is not "locked" or in any other mode that doesn't allow programming to happen.

6. Open the Programming Software

- Run the programming tools that you set up earlier. To use CHIRP, open the program and pick your radio type from the list of radios that it supports.
- If you're using software made by the manufacturer, choose your radio model and set up the settings by following the program's directions.

7. Select the Correct COM Port (for Windows Users)

- Sometimes you may need to choose the right COM port by hand when the programming wire is plugged in. Check the Device Manager on your computer (Windows) to find this.
- If you're using CHIRP, it might find the right COM port for you immediately. In that case, pick the correct port from the list of choices.

8. Prepare the Radio for Data Transfer

- You might have to put some radios into programming mode by hand. Usually, you can do this by hitting a certain button or holding down a group of buttons (check the user instructions for your radio for more information).
- For instance, to get into programming mode on a Baofeng radio, you might have to press the "**Menu**" button and then a certain key.

You can start programming your GMRS radio with the settings you want as soon as it is turned on, linked to the computer, and the software is ready.

Programming Frequencies in the Radio

After getting your computer and GMRS radio ready for programming, the next step is to set your radio to the right frequencies. To do this, you need to give the exact GMRS channels and frequencies you want to use for talking.

1. Access the Programming Mode

- Make sure the radio is turned on.
- If your radio has a Programming Mode, press a certain key or set of buttons to get into it. On a lot of Baofeng radios, for instance, you would press the Menu button and then go to the settings for programming.
- If you're using software like CHIRP, you don't have to go into programming mode by hand; once you connect the software to the radio, it will do it for you.

2. Connect the Radio to Your Computer

- Connect your radio to your computer with the programming cord. When you use a USB-to-serial connection, make sure the drivers are set up properly.
- On your computer, open the programming software, such as CHIRP or software made by the maker.

3. Pick the Right COM Port and Radio Model

- Choose the right radio type in the software to make sure it works.
- Make sure you choose the right COM port. If you're using Windows, you can check this in the Device Manager to make sure the software is talking to the right port.

4. Download or Read the Current Settings

- It's a good idea to read the current settings of your radio into the software before adding new frequencies. You can easily view and back up any current programming this way.
- In the software, click on the Read from Radio button. This will move the radio's current settings to the software, where you can change them.

5. Put in GMRS frequencies

- GMRS frequencies typically fall within the 462-467 MHz range, and your programming software should provide you with a list of these frequencies.
- Manually input the desired frequencies into the software. You can either:
  - **Enter each frequency manually** in the frequency list.
  - **Use pre-programmed GMRS channels** (e.g., CHIRP includes predefined GMRS frequencies).
- You may need to enter the **channel name**, such as "GMRS Channel 1" for each frequency, depending on your software.

Here's an example of the basic GMRS channels you might use:

- Channel 1: 462.5500 MHz (GMRS)
- Channel 2: 462.5750 MHz (GMRS)
- Channel 3: 462.6000 MHz (GMRS)
- Channel 4: 462.6250 MHz (GMRS)
- (And so on...)

6. Set Privacy Codes (Optional)

- You don't have to use privacy codes, which are also known as CTCSS or DCS codes, but they can be helpful if you want to control who can hear your messages.
- In the tools for programming, you can give each channel its own privacy code. This is especially helpful for GMRS radios so that other people on the same channel don't mess with them.

7. Set the Power Output and Other Settings (Optional)

- Depending on the software and the radio model, you can also adjust settings like:
  - **Power output** (high or low)
  - **Squelch levels**
  - **Tone settings**

8. Write the Settings to the Radio

- After entering the frequencies and settings you want, it's time to send the changes back to the radio.
- Go to your software and click on Write to Radio or a similar button. This will make the GMRS radio use the new frequencies and settings that were saved on the computer.

9. Test the Radio

- Turn on the radio after pulling it away from the computer and programming the frequencies.
- Transmit and receive signals on various channels to test the frequencies. Depending on where you are and what you like, you may need to change the noise levels or other settings.

Troubleshooting Common Programming Issues

1. Radio Not Recognized by the Software

One of the most typical problems is that the programming software doesn't see the radio. This could be because of a number of things:

- **Wrong Cable or Connection**: Make sure that the programming cable is plugged into both the computer and the radio in the right way. When using a USB-to-serial adapter, make sure the wire link is strong and stable.
- **Outdated or Missing Drivers**: The programming cord may need certain drivers to let the radio and computer talk to each other. You should get these drivers from the website of the maker and install them. To use a USB-to-serial connection, you might need the FTDI or Prolific drivers.
- **COM Port Configuration**: The program might not be connected to the right COM port. In Windows, open Device Manager and look at the list of current COM ports. Make sure that the programming software is set up to use the correct one. In the Device Manager, a yellow question mark next to your wire means there is a problem with the driver.
- **Problems with Other Software**: Other apps that use serial connections can sometimes cause problems. Do not run any other programs that use serial ports.

2. Unable to Write Data to the Radio

There could be problems when you try to write new settings to the radio. That being said, there are a few things that might be causing this:

- **Radio in the Wrong Mode**: To send data, many radios need to be in Programming Mode. Check the instructions for your radio to make sure you're in the right mode. Take the Baofeng radio as an example. To get into programming mode, you might need to press the Menu button and then another key.
- **Low Battery**: If the radio doesn't have enough power, it might not accept the new settings. Before you try to set up your radio, you should always make sure it is fully charged or has new batteries.
- **Incompatible Software or Firmware**: Some radios can only work with certain types of programming software or firmware. Make sure you're using the right software version for your radio type and firmware version.
- **Trouble Connecting**: Make sure the wire is firmly attached to both the computer and the radio. If you're having trouble connecting a USB-to-serial cord, try a different USB port on your computer or a different adapter.

3. Frequencies Not Saving After Programming

When you enter frequencies, the radio might not always save them correctly. This problem could be caused by a number of things:

- **Wrong Power Down**: The settings might not be saved if the radio is turned off or removed too soon. Before you turn off the radio or disconnect the wire, you should always wait for the programming process to finish.
- **Glitches in the Software**: The programming software may sometimes have a glitch or bug that stops frequencies from being saved correctly. Check to see if you have the most recent version of the software. You might want to try again after restarting both the radio and the program.
- **Memory Limits**: Some radios can only store a certain number of frequencies in their memory. If you try to put in more frequencies than the radio can hold, it might not be able to handle them all. Check to see how much memory your model has and make sure you're not going over it.
- **Writing to the Wrong Slot**: If the software lets you write multiple channels, make sure you're writing the frequencies to the right channel spot. Make sure that the program shows that the channels are filled with the right frequencies.

4. Radio Not Transmitting or Receiving Signals

After programming the frequencies, your radio may fail to transmit or receive signals. Several factors could be contributing to this issue:

- **Incorrect Frequency**: Double-check that the frequencies programmed into your radio are correct. GMRS radios use specific frequency ranges, so ensure that you're within the proper range (462.5500 MHz to 467.7250 MHz). If you input a frequency outside this range, the radio will not transmit or receive properly.
- **Privacy Codes (CTCSS/DCS)**: If you're using privacy codes (CTCSS or DCS), ensure they are set correctly. These codes filter out unwanted transmissions and may block communication if mismatched. If you're unable to hear anyone on a channel, try disabling the privacy codes to test whether they're the cause.

- **Power Output Settings**: Some radios have adjustable power output settings, allowing you to choose between low or high power. If the radio is set to low power, it may not transmit far enough to be heard. Set the radio to high power if you're trying to communicate over longer distances.
- **Antenna Issues**: The antenna might not be properly connected or could be damaged. Ensure the antenna is securely attached and in good condition for optimal signal transmission.

5. Software Crashes or Freezes

While programming the radio, the software may freeze or crash unexpectedly, which can be caused by various reasons:

- **Incompatible Software or Version**: Ensure that the software version is compatible with your radio model. Check the software's documentation to verify this. If you're using an older version of the software, it may not fully support newer radios or firmware.
- **System Resources**: If your computer is running low on memory or processing power, the programming software may become unstable. Try closing unnecessary programs or restarting your computer before attempting to program the radio again.
- **Corrupt Files**: Sometimes, the configuration file being used to store the programming information becomes corrupted. If this happens, try creating a new file or reinstalling the software to eliminate any corrupt files.

6. Radio Display Shows Errors After Programming

If the radio shows an error message or a garbled display after programming, it's likely a sign of one of the following:

- **Firmware Mismatch**: The radio's firmware may not be compatible with the programming software or settings. If you're using third-party software, check whether the software supports the latest firmware of your radio model. Updating the radio's firmware may resolve the issue.

- **Corrupted Data**: The data on the radio may have been corrupted during the programming process. To resolve this, you may need to reset the radio to factory settings and reprogram it from scratch.
- **Faulty Software or Cable**: The issue could stem from a faulty cable or incompatible software. Try using a different cable or updating the software.

7. Interference from Other Radio Signals

Even after programming your radio correctly, you might experience interference from other signals, making communication difficult:

- **Signal Congestion**: If you're operating in an area with many other GMRS or similar radio users, channels may be congested. Try selecting a different channel or frequency to avoid interference.
- **Poor Signal Reception**: In some areas, especially in cities or heavily wooded areas, the signal may be weak. Consider adjusting the antenna or testing the radio in an open area for better signal reception.

CHAPTER 7

ADVANCED GMRS FEATURES AND FUNCTIONS

GPS Integration

GPS (Global Positioning System) functions can enhance the use of GMRS (General Mobile Radio Service) radios by allowing users to exchange and track their position information. This link is especially useful when it's critical to know exactly where team members are, such as on an outdoor excursion, reacting to an emergency, or at work.

1. Location Tracking: GMRS radios with GPS can track each device's location and display it on a map in real-time. This feature is extremely useful when knowing exactly where each team member is is critical to safety and coordination. It increases your awareness of your environment, allowing you to communicate and plan more effectively.

2. Waypoint Navigation: These radios with built-in GPS systems allow users to create waypoints, which are precise locations that can be found by their respective numbers. Waypoint navigation allows users to design routes, mark essential locations, and direct others on a team to specific destinations. This capability is especially useful for outdoor sports, exploration, and situations requiring precise navigation.

3. Emergency Alerts: In an emergency, GMRS radios equipped with GPS can communicate both distress signals and the user's current position, allowing aid to be dispatched. This functionality is critical for rapid and precise replies, particularly in situations when traditional modes of communication may be impossible or unreliable.

4. **Geo-Fencing:** Geo-fencing is the process of creating virtual borders on a map. GPS-enabled GMRS radios can send out warnings or notifications when a device crosses certain boundaries. This tool can assist you in creating safe zones, monitoring people's movements in certain locations, and ensuring that they adhere to the boundaries that have been established.

5. Location Sharing: Users can actively communicate their real-time location with other team members equipped with GPS-enabled GMRS radios. This motivates individuals to make choices collectively, makes it simpler to meet in certain locations, and enhances overall teamwork.

6. Mapping Software Compatibility: Adding mapping software or applications enhances the visual representation of geographical data. This compatibility allows users to layer GPS data on top of comprehensive maps, providing a more complete image of their surroundings, routes, and markers.

7. Search and Rescue Operations: GPS is extremely useful for search and rescue operations. It allows teams to better coordinate and cover defined search regions, reducing the time it takes to discover persons in difficulty. When communication and location information are merged, a large number of lives can be saved.

Before purchasing GMRS radios with GPS built-in, thoroughly review the device's specifications to ensure it fulfills your unique requirements. Also, those who use GMRS radios should be aware of any additional fees, services, or permits required to use the GPS functions.

Weather Alerts and NOAA Channels

Many contemporary **FRS (Family Radio Service), GMRS (General Mobile Radio Service),** and **CB (Citizens Band)** radios have NOAA weather channels, which are extremely useful to their users. Well-known brands like Cobra, Garmin, Midland, Motorola, Olympia, and Uniden all produce models with NOAA weather channels that provide users with real-time weather information and warnings. Here's how these NOAA weather channels function and how to utilize them on two-way radios or radios designed specifically for emergency situations:

The NOAA weather channels employ seven distinct radio frequencies in the VHF (Very High Frequency) band. These frequencies are solely used to deliver weather updates, alerts, and warnings across the United States. The network of antennas ensures that critical meteorological information is distributed 24 hours a day, seven days a week, 365 days a year. Some two-way radios may additionally have three additional weather channels, with two of them reserved for Canadian maritime weather bulletins.

NOAA Weather Frequencies

Here are the seven NOAA weather frequencies that have been set aside:

1. 162.400 MHz
2. 162.425 MHz
3. 162.450 MHz
4. 162.475 MHz
5. 162.500 MHz
6. 162.525 MHz
7. 162.550 MHz

It can be difficult to determine which channel to use for weather frequencies on two-way radios because there is no standard procedure. The 162.400 MHz weather frequency may be assigned to Channel 1 on one radio model but Channel 4 on another. Radio manufacturers decide how to assign channels and weather frequencies. Although this range of frequencies may appear perplexing, the owner's handbook for your radio can typically assist you find out which frequency is on which channel.

Most manufacturers' manuals offer a list or table of weather frequency channels as well as instructions on how to access them. Different radios may have different channel allocations, but the instructions will show you how to properly set up your device.

The National Weather Service (NWS) is an excellent resource for determining the most essential weather frequency for your organization. A complete list of all the frequencies used by weather stations in the United States can be found on the NOAA Weather Radio All Hazards website.

It is possible to find the NWS station that is closest to you in two ways:

1. **NWS Nationwide Station Listing Using Broadcast Frequencies:**

   o Go to the NWS website and find the Nationwide Station Listing Using Broadcast Frequencies page.

- o Click on your state, find the name of the area that is nearest to you on the list, and write down the call sign and frequency that go with it.
- o When you click on the call sign, you will be taken to a new page with more information about the station and a map showing where it broadcasts.

2. **NWR Transmitter Search:**

   - o Go to the NWS website and look for NWR transmitters.
   - o Type the name of your city or state into the search box.
   - o Clicking on the icon on the map will give you information about the station near where you are.

Once you know what frequency the broadcaster uses in your location, you can easily access the weather channels on your radio. First, utilize the channel assignments in your owner's manual to locate the radio channel that is programmed to the NOAA weather frequency you discovered. Once you've located it, follow the instructions in your owner's manual to switch on the channel. To switch on, most radios need you to navigate the menu or settings and choose the weather channel.

Always consult your owner's handbook for clear, model-specific instructions. It will show you step by step how to access the weather channels and enable weather alerts on your individual radio model and manufacture.

If you follow these instructions, your radio will be prepared to receive NOAA weather forecasts and broadcasts. Remember that the precise procedures may change depending on the radio type, which is why it is critical to read the owner's handbook thoroughly.

Encryption and Privacy

Hackers and others are unable to comprehend encoded information, but those who should be able to do so can. This process is referred to as encryption. Encryption in two-way radios alters a voice stream through the application of coding algorithms.

An encryption key instructs this software what to perform. It is the encryption key that both transmit and receive radios utilize to encode and decode speech data. To receive communications, all radios communicating with one another must have identical encryption keys.

GMRS Encryption helps keep users' private and essential data out of the hands of others who shouldn't view it by employing an extremely secure kind of encryption. GMRS Encryption's powerful encryption technology makes it an excellent choice for protecting personal information and preventing accidental data theft. This strategy is increasingly being utilized in industries such as government, healthcare, and finance to ensure the integrity of their data.

Get to Know GMRS Encryption: What You Need to Know

General Mobile Radio System (GMRS) encryption is a sort of digital radio technology that is used to secure two-way radio communications. It accomplishes this by scrambling radio frequencies and encrypting communications, allowing the sender and receiver to communicate securely. This prevents those who are listening to signs from picking them up and deciphering them.

When GMRS encryption is used for two-way radio communication, a variety of positive outcomes occur.

- The gadget is simple to operate and requires only a connection to existing GMRS radios.
- This option is cost-effective as it does not require any additional equipment.
- Provides a secure solution for VHF or UHF radio systems that do not employ encryption.
- It increases radio signal quality and reduces congestion and signal loss.

General Mobile Radio System (GMRS) encryption can be utilized in a wide range of radio technologies, including private radios, public safety radios, and military radios. GMRS encryption might be effective for high-risk situations, intelligence collection, and private data transmission. This is because it allows individuals who use two-way radios to communicate in a safe and secure manner while maintaining confidence.

Deciphering the Secrets of GMRS Encryption

It may appear like decrypting GMRS is a difficult process, but if you know what you're doing, it may not be so bad! To understand how to crack the GMRS encryption, here's how it works:

- **RCS (Root Code Set) Decryption**: The "Root Code Set" is the starting point for GMRS encryption. The code is made up of twenty-character keys that must be deciphered to reveal the secret contents.

- **Symmetric Keys:** GMRS encryption users can utilize symmetric keys to authenticate themselves. Everyone who uses the system requires a unique key, which must be kept somewhere safe so that no one else can access the encrypted communications.
- **Asymmetric Keys:** Asymmetric keys are often used for encryption and decryption. They are longer and safer than symmetric keys and are used to decrypt compressed communications. They can also be used to return texts.

By studying the basics first, you will be able to investigate the many methods of GMRS encryption. This category includes methods like obfuscation, masking, hashing, salting, and more. If you completely understand these strategies, you will be able to read the encrypted communications and secure your data.

Becoming a GMRS Encryption Pro

Decipher the Basics

There is a sort of internet security called GMRS encryption. This system consists of two parts: the key and the breaker algorithm. The breaker algorithm converts a signal to an unknown value. The key is similar to a password and is used to decode encrypted data. The first step towards becoming a professional is to grasp the fundamentals.

- Learning the basics of coding is important.
- You should also understand what a breaker algorithm is and
- Be familiar with a lot of different codes and encryption methods that the GMRS system can use.

Develop Advanced Skills

Once you're certain you grasp the fundamentals, it's time to put your abilities to the test. Learning about the most recent encryption methods and algorithms employed by the GMRS system is critical. Learn to utilize them. You may find the following things interesting:

- Create encrypted data contact routes and be in charge of managing them.
- If you're in the real world, you should use encryption software.
- Make sure that websites and web apps are safe to use.
- Look at the security architecture that is already in place on a website or app.

Unlocking the Benefits of GMRS Encryption

When it comes to protecting digital communications, General Mobile Radio Service (GMRS) encryption is the most effective. GMRS provides consumers with increased security due to greater encryption, improved authentication, and more consistent system stability. Here are the four most significant reasons to adopt GMRS encryption:

- **Secure Communications:** GMRS encryption ensures secure and private network connections for voice, video, and data. In this manner, users can be confident that only those who are authorized will be able to view the information they are attempting to share.
- **Enhanced Authentication:** GMRS encryption improves authentication by checking identities, ensuring passwords are accurate, and retaining session logs to reduce the likelihood that someone will try to hack or modify them.
- **Increased System Security:** GMRS encryption improves system security by using better encryption algorithms. These actions protect user information from theft, assaults, and unauthorized access.

- **Improved Legitimacy**: GMRS encryption can verify long-distance transactions and linkages. This ensures that messages are from legitimate and trustworthy sources.

Companies can safeguard their networks and communications against risks such as theft, hacking, and assault by including GMRS encryption in their data and voice security choices. Users can be certain that their discussions, documents, movies, and other sensitive data are secure thanks to increased security and authentication protocols.

Encrypting voice signals

Voice messages can be encrypted in some different ways.

Simple Inversion Encryption

Inversion scrambling involves switching the frequencies and loudness of a spoken signal. On the left side of Figure 1, all 300Hz voice signal frequencies have been reversed to 3kHz. Also, the volume is set backward. Most two-way radios that can flip the sound have 32 encryption keys to choose from.

To configure the radio's keys, utilize radio setting software. People in close proximity to radios that utilize the same frequency, have the same privacy code and encryption key, and are within range of your signal will be able to hear your communications. For the majority of two-way radio users, this level of encryption is enough. Many low-end and mid-range radios already have this type of encryption built in.

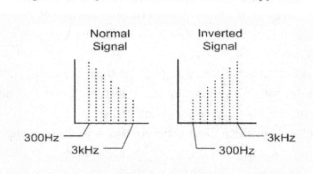

Fig. 1 - Simple Voice Inversion Encryption

Hopping Inversion Encryption

It is safer to utilize frequency hopping encryption rather than basic inversion. Figure 2 indicates that when this strategy is utilized, the frequencies and frequency rates shift unexpectedly. As a result, the sound signal "hops" between frequencies and frequency levels. This technology has been implemented in certain commercial radios on the 900MHz band, but not in the majority of them.

Fig. 2 - Frequency Hopping Encryption

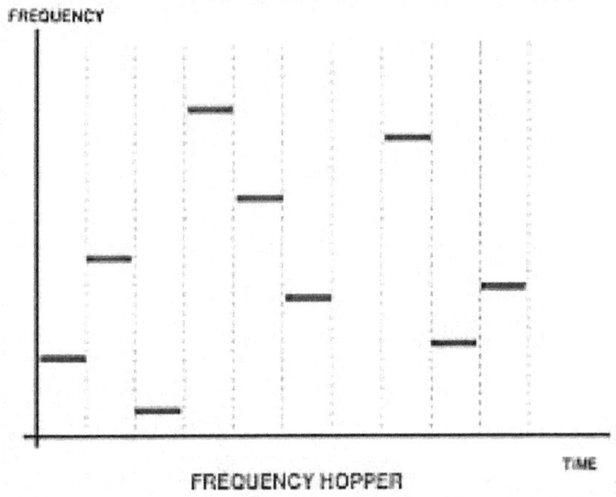

FREQUENCY

FREQUENCY HOPPER

TIME

Rolling Code Inversion Encryption

Rolling code inversion involves turning the sound signal around at a variable rate over time. Figure 3: On the left, you can see that the signal begins at an upward inversion frequency and progresses to the maximum level. Then it goes the other way, inverting at lower frequencies until it reaches the lower limit. Simple voice inversion is less secure than this sort of encryption. Most radios that support rolling code encryption have 1020 encryption keys. Scripting software configures the radio keys.

Fig. 3 - Rolling Code Encryption

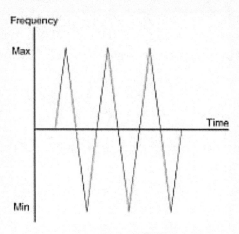

Radios within the range that utilize the same frequency, privacy code, and encryption key will be able to hear your communications. There are two forms of inversion: basic and rolling. The number of codes (1020 for rolling) and the "rolling" inversion of the signal make rolling codes more difficult to break. Rolling code is utilized in more significant applications. Some mid-range radios and the most advanced radios can have rolling code encryption as an option.

DES and AES Encryption

Some banking apps, the FBI, and other sensitive systems employ either AES (Advanced Encryption Standard) or DES (Data Encryption Standard), a relative of AES. Even though DES was developed in the 1970s, its relative AES has taken its place in a variety of applications. These encryption algorithms are rather sophisticated, and understanding them requires a strong background in arithmetic and cryptography. This is the "gold standard" in encryption. However, exactly like actual gold, they are more difficult to utilize and cost more to apply.

Setting the encryption keys for AES and DES is likewise quite delicate because they are utilized for highly sensitive jobs. The numbers must be set using "keyloader" (also known as "KVL") devices. It resembles a radio, and it allows the user to insert the keys into the encryption boards within. A unique wire links the KVL to the radio and its interface port.

Depending on the protocol, the operator enters various numbers and letters into the KVL to generate a unique code for your radio data. The KVL converts your code, which consists of around 20 characters, into the final key that is subsequently programmed into each radio. Because entering the KVL implies entering the entire system, these devices are not accessible to the public and are highly secured at radio shops or government offices where they are housed.

Managing Encryption Keys in a Complex Environment

So, how do you update the encryption keys when you have so much work to perform? Over-the-air rekeying, or OTAR, is the solution. In OTAR, a unique computer known as a **Key Management Controller (KMC)** manages all encryption keys from a single location. The term originates from the fact that OTAR allows radios to receive fresh encryption keys over the air. You can also erase encryption keys wirelessly.

If one of the system's radios is lost or stolen, it can be re-keyed remotely. Also, if you accidentally remove your radio's batteries and destroy the encryption key, the KMC can send the key back over the air. The KMC can also store encryption keys in KVLs, allowing them to be sent. If the radios are too far away for the KMC to reach, the KVL can be utilized instead.

Many radios can only hold one key for encryption at a time. However, certain radios can hold more than one encryption key, a feature known as "multi-key." Multi-key allows individuals with both encryption keys in their radios to communicate with both groups while the remainder of the group is unable to listen in. This is handy if you have two distinct groups with different encryption keys. Some radios with multiple keys can hold up to 16 distinct encryption keys.

OTAR and multi-key are often only found on more sophisticated radios.

Compatibility of Encryption Between Different Brands

Many people want to know if multiple radio brands' encryption can be used together. The only common encryption algorithms are AES and DES. In other words, separate two-way radios can support both AES and DES.

However, there are no universally accepted criteria for basic or rolling code inversion encryption. Each manufacturer can create their own codes and techniques to jumble them for both simple and rolling code inversion. This implies that basic inversion and rolling code inversion encryption are rarely compatible between brands.

CHAPTER 8

INTEGRATION WITH OTHER RADIO SYSTEMS

Compatibility with FRS Radios

In recent years, various manufacturers have created "high-power" radios for public usage. These radios are touted as communication equipment for families or recreational activities, and they are available as impulse purchases at department stores. In addition to boasting a few miles of range, they may be powered by a rechargeable battery pack or AA batteries, and the majority of them are surprisingly sturdy and simple to operate.

FRS and GMRS technology are responsible for these extensively used radios. Both of these types of radios are available in similar packaging and are regularly found on adjacent shelves; nevertheless, their capabilities and operating restrictions differ significantly.

FRS

In 1996, the Federal Communications Commission (FCC) authorized the use of Family Radio Service, often known as FRS, without a license. The phrase "UHF Citizens Band" is occasionally used to refer to the frequency range of 462 to 467 MHz. Unlike 802.11 radios, which are governed by FCC Part 15, this device is monitored by FCC Part 95, designated "**Personal Radio Services.**"

GMRS and FRS radios share multiple channels, however the maximum power that FRS radios can output is 500 milliwatts. According to the manufacturers, the maximum range of FRS radios is typically two miles. FRS radios frequently come fitted with fixed antennas, and it is illegal to alter them to accommodate antennas or amplifiers.

To communicate with GMRS radios, use FRS channels 1-7, which overlap with GMRS channels. If you simply need to connect with other FRS radios and want to prevent potential interference with low-band GMRS users, use channels 8 through 14.

GMRS

GMRS Handheld Device Although handhelds with a power output of 4 Watts are more common, GMRS devices can generate up to 5 Watts of electricity. Fixed-base stations can use up to 15 Watts of power on most frequencies; however, they can only utilize 5 Watts of power when communicating on FRS channels. The maximum strength that repeater stations can broadcast is fifty watts.

Handhelds can communicate on any GMRS frequency, however, fixed-base stations and repeaters can only transmit on the lower "462" frequencies. GMRS equipment may have detachable antennas, allowing you to use a portable device with either a car mount or a fixed antenna. The General Mobile Radio Service (GMRS) can facilitate communication over long distances by using repeaters.

The entire list of frequencies for both the FRS and GMRS can be seen below.

Lower frequency	Upper frequency	Purpose
462.550	467.550	GMRS "550"
462.5625	—	FRS channel 1, GMRS "5625"
462.575	467.575	GMRS "575"
462.5875	—	FRS channel 2, GMRS "5875"
462.600	467.600	GMRS "600"
462.6125	—	FRS channel 3, GMRS "6125"
462.625	467.625	GMRS "625"
462.6375	—	FRS channel 4, GMRS "6375"
462.650	467.650	GMRS "650"
462.6625	—	FRS channel 5, GMRS "6625"
462.675	467.675	GMRS "675"
462.6875	—	FRS channel 6, GMRS "6875"

462.700	467.700	GMRS "700"
462.7125	—	FRS channel 7, GMRS "7125"
462.725	467.725	GMRS "725"
467.5625	—	FRS channel 8
467.5875	—	FRS channel 9
467.6125	—	FRS channel 10
467.6375	—	FRS channel 11
467.6625	—	FRS channel 12
467.6875	—	FRS channel 13
467.7125	—	FRS channel 14

Generally, portable GMRS devices communicate with one another at lower frequencies wherever possible. When talking with a repeater, they transmit on higher frequencies while listening to lower frequencies at 5 MHz. As a result, anyone listening on the "462" side can hear both handheld device traffic and repeater transmission.

To avoid unnecessary interference with other GMRS users, use lower frequencies and power levels wherever possible. Only utilize repeaters when you can't make contact in any other manner.

Extending Range

Even having radios with higher power outputs can help you extend your range slightly, the most effective method to do so is to increase your height. Even when the antenna is high in the air, UHF radios can go much further than they would otherwise, even with little power. Part 95 laws limit "small control stations" to antennas no higher than twenty feet above the structure to which they are fastened.

This is one of the reasons these restrictions exist. When transmitting, it is best to be on high ground to get the most out of your FRS or GMRS radio. In some cases, this can significantly increase the useful range. A GMRS radio's effective range may be substantially increased by attaching it to a tall antenna, just like any other radio.

Although these radios can only transmit a limited amount of data and operate in half duplex mode, they are helpful in a number of situations. For example, you may realize that they are significantly more useful than mobile phones when it comes to fine-tuning a long-distance point-to-point 802.11 network.

When operating in distant areas, particularly on hills and mountains, FRS and GMRS radios may be a significantly more dependable mode of communication than a phone. On the other hand, you should not have any clever ideas like connecting a radio to a telephone patch because this is not authorized by the FRS or the GMRS.

Utilizing FRS and GMRS Radios for Local Disaster Communication

Certain disasters have the potential to interrupt the communication infrastructure we take for granted and utilize every day. If there are too many idle phones, the local phone system may get overwhelmed. This can happen when an earthquake rattles the phone lines or when a large number of people try to call worried friends and family.

Furthermore, if there are too many individuals trying to make calls on their mobile phones, the system may come to a total halt. Furthermore, our telephones may become useless if the infrastructure is destroyed.

Because of the widespread availability of small handheld radios that are part of the Family Radio Service (FRS) and the General Mobile Radio Service (GMRS), these radios have become a popular choice for providing backup communications during neighborhood crises. There are benefits to this popularity, such as lower pricing and widespread availability. However, it comes at a cost: an overwhelming number of users on a very limited number of frequencies sometimes referred to as "**channels**." (If you find yourself in Disneyland, try listening to an FRS station!)

The good news is that your FRS or GMRS radio will not be able to receive signals from all other users in Los Angeles. Because of their low power and small antennas, these radios have a restricted effective range, which can be as little as a few blocks at times. Intervening buildings and terrain may also have an impact on their communication range.

In general, transmissions from your immediate neighbors will be stronger than those from a mile or two distant. This is because the signal strength between two such radios rises proportionally with their closeness to one another. As a result, they may be an excellent alternative for use by small teams working on utility shutdowns, checking on neighbors with special needs, and performing other similar chores.

Tone encoders and decoders are built into the majority of FRS and GMRS radios. These components may be referred to as "privacy code," "PL," or other related terminology. This feature, which acts as an audio filter, allows the transmitter to broadcast an inaudible tone anytime the transmit button is touched, and it also causes the receiver to keep the audio quiet until it receives a signal containing that tone.

The goal is to avoid listening to communications that were not intended for you. You should ideally only hear the party on the other end of the connection, whose radio is set to the same channel and privacy code that you have already agreed upon.

It is crucial to remember that this function has no effect on privacy; anyone listening to your channel whose radio has the tone feature turned off can hear every word you broadcast, regardless of whether the tone is there. Furthermore, the signal from another radio station on your channel may be louder than the signal from the person you intend to connect with, obscuring your receiver. You simply would not be able to hear it, or anything else, until the other radio ceased transmitting that signal.

Amateur radio operators, sometimes known as "**hams**," can communicate over longer distances than FRS and GMRS. They can reach across the entire country and town by using the necessary equipment and picking appropriate frequencies. Because of the more strict communication standards, each town benefits from having several hams nearby. A local amateur radio club or a neighborhood ham may be able to give you further information; you can also ask about it on the website areslax.org.

The ownership of radios is advantageous, but the skill to utilize them efficiently is a critical component of communication. Remember to keep your radios' batteries fresh (alkaline) or well-charged (rechargeable), and have replacements on hand so you can get the most out of them. During the planning phase, you should agree on who will use which channels (and, for neighborhood use, privacy codes), as well as have backup channels in case one of the channels is interfered with by other signals. In the case of a crisis, practice using your radios in the exact areas where you will use them.

When broadcasting, speak slowly and clearly into the microphone, keeping it one to two inches away from your mouth. Also, avoid shouting. You should try to avoid areas with a lot of background noise since it will make it more difficult for the other person to understand you and for you to hear him. The fire department, police department, and military all employ **TACTICAL CALLSIGNS** on their radio equipment. These signals are frequently associated with a certain function or area.

First names may be OK for a limited number of users, but they may cause confusion when there are many people on the same channel. For example, the utilities team you have may choose to use "**Utility One**," "**Utility Two**," and so on. Your strategy must include any tactical callsigns you intend to utilize. The habit of opening each conversation with a statement from the party you intend to contact, followed by your own call ("Supply, this is Triage") is seen as excellent practice.

You should not send your message until you receive an acknowledgment that says "Triage, Supply, go ahead." To avoid leaving the other party waiting to see if you have anything else to say, keep your communications brief ("Supply, Triage, we need six blankets at Elm & 1st right away") and sign off when the exchange is complete ("Triage clear"). This will allow the other party to resume their other responsibilities. Last but not least, do not underestimate the value of non-radio ways of communication. Amazingly, youngsters who ride bicycles or scooters may travel from one block to the next in a short period of time.

Connect to GMRS Repeaters Around You

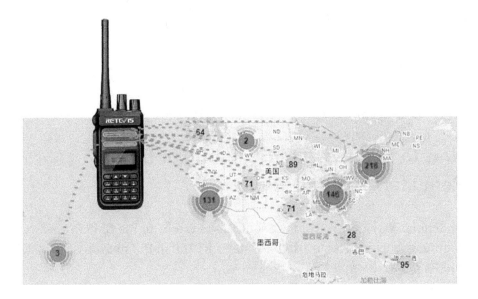

It is feasible to use GMRS radio to connect GMRS repeaters and obtain a longer calling distance. With your GMRS radios, you may either buy your own GMRS repeaters or link them to open GMRS repeaters owned by others.

How to Find Open GMRS Repeaters Around Me

We can get a lot of public GMRS repeater information on MYGMRS (website: mygmrs.com) and ARKANSAN REPEATER GROUP (website: https://arkradio.net/repeaters/) in addition to other General Mobile Radio Service (GMRS) websites. This public information will allow you to discover more about the GMRS repeater situation in your region. After gaining approval, you can contact the owner of the repeater and link it. After that, you may connect your GMRS radio to these GMRS repeaters to increase communication range. Today, we will use the Retevis RT76P as an example to show how to connect your GMRS radio to your preferred GMRS repeater.

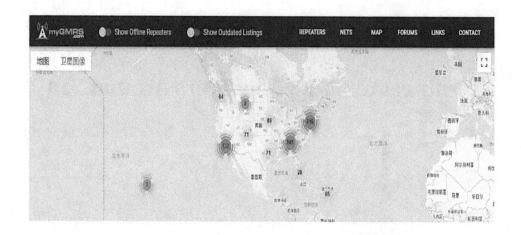

How to Connect a GMRS Radio to GMRS Repeaters Around You

To demonstrate how to connect your GMRS radios to the GMRS repeaters in your neighborhood, let us use the Retevis RT76P GMRS two-way radio, RT97, and RT97S as examples.

Step 1: Know the RX, TX, B/N, and Tone Out/In of the Repeater Around you, that you want to Connect to.

For example, on the website https://mygmrs.com/map, you may get the following information about a GMRS repeater near you:

be asked to leave the repeater or you will be reported to the FCC..

frecuencia- L 462.625 - H 467.625

Repetidor Paso-12.50K

transmisión TX- DPL es 131 Hz In/Out.

If you wish, you can inform me about the work and performance of the transmission as well as its location. liahju06@yahoo.com.

The H frequency is 467.625 megahertz, the L frequency is 462.625 megahertz, and the B/N ratio is 12.50 kilohertz, indicating "**n**" or narrow (B = 25 kilohertz). In addition, the Tone Out/In ratio is 131.

Step 2: Prepare the Retevis RT76P Gmrs Two-Way Radio and the Program Cable, and then Connect Them to the Computer.

After reading, we will notice that the Retevis RT76P has 26 channels, with the TX frequency 467.625 and the RX frequency 462.625. This frequency corresponds to the left-hand frequency of a nearby GMRS repeater.

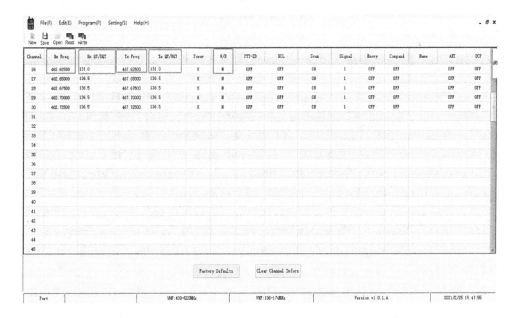

The only thing we need to do is use the wire to directly input the 26-channel Rx QT/DQT and Rx QT/DQT (the repeater's Tone Out/In) into 131. Furthermore, the repeater repetidor paso 12.50KZ indicates that the selected B/N is N (as previously stated).

Once the settings have been confirmed as correct, they should be stored on the Retevis RT76P radio. After successfully completing the write process, you will be able to enhance the talking distance of your Retevis RT76P by using the shared repeater. The specific extendable distance is decided by both the environment in which your walkie-talkie is utilized and the circumstances around the repeater. Take the required steps to guarantee that your GMRs radio is in range of the GMRs repeater signal.

Cross-Band Operations and Interoperability

Cross-band operation and communication are critical components of the General Mobile Radio Service (GMRS), allowing users to communicate with one another without difficulty utilizing different devices and frequency bands. This feature increases the adaptability and utility of GMRS communication, allowing users to avoid potential difficulties and collaborate more effectively. Understanding the rules and procedures of cross-band operation increases the GMRS network's flexibility and ability to interact with other networks.

GMRS radios can transmit and receive messages over many frequency bands. This is known as "**cross-band operation.**" Users will find this capability extremely useful when they need to communicate with persons or organizations whose radios use different bands than theirs. It provides different radio users greater flexibility and allows them to collaborate, so they can build up contact lines across several frequencies.

Interoperability in GMRS implies that radios of different brands or types can communicate without issue. This promotes compatibility and collaboration. Interoperability is critical for emergency situations, public safety, and other scenarios in which individuals may need to use a range of radio instruments. Standards and standards developed by organizations such as the Telecommunications Industry Association (TIA) and the Electronic Industries Alliance (EIA) are critical for enabling connection.

- Understand frequency ranges for effective cross-band operation and communication in GMRS. They should learn the specific frequency bands that can be utilized for GMRS. This involves becoming familiar with the primary GMRS channels as well as any additional bands designated for particular or combined usage.
- Program GMRS radios with appropriate frequencies and tones for cross-band communication. This might involve manually configuring radios or utilizing software tools provided by the manufacturer.
- Use tone squelch capabilities, such as CTCSS or DCS, to reduce interference and promote privacy during conversations. These characteristics can be quite beneficial in cross-band scenarios when many groups are functioning concurrently.

- Ensure everyone talking between bands has a current GMRS license. It is critical to obey the regulations established by authorities such as the Federal Communications Commission (FCC) in order to remain lawful and avoid potential penalties.
- Test and train radios to ensure they can communicate across multiple bands. This preventative strategy helps to identify issues and ensures that users understand how to function across bands.
- When purchasing new GMRS devices, choose compatible equipment that supports cross-band operation and fulfills industry requirements. A more dependable communication network consists of components that can function together and are manufactured by well-known firms.

CHAPTER 9

TROUBLESHOOTING AND MAINTENANCE

Common GMRS Radio Issues and Solutions

1. Poor Signal Reception.

Problem: Weak or unclear signals can occur, making it difficult to hear others or be heard clearly.

Solution:

- **Check Antenna**: Ensure the antenna is properly connected and not damaged. A damaged or improperly connected antenna can significantly reduce signal strength.
- **Change Location**: If you're in a dense area with many obstructions (such as buildings or trees), try moving to a more open area. GMRS radios operate best in open spaces with a clear line of sight.
- **Increase Power**: If your radio allows for power selection, switch to a higher power mode for a stronger signal. Keep in mind that higher power consumes more battery.
- **Use a Repeater**: If you're in a mountainous or remote area, consider using a repeater to extend your range. Repeaters can help amplify the signal, increasing the communication distance.

2. Battery Draining Quickly

Problem: The battery runs out much faster than expected.

Solution:

- **Turn Off Unnecessary Features**: Features like **VOX (Voice-Activated Transmission)**, **backlighting**, or **dual watch** can drain the battery faster. Turn off features you don't need.
- **Reduce Transmission Time**: Long or frequent transmissions can drain the battery quickly. Limit the length of your conversations and avoid holding down the PTT (Push-to-Talk) key unnecessarily.

- **Use Rechargeable Batteries**: Opt for high-quality, rechargeable batteries designed for GMRS radios, as these tend to last longer than disposable batteries. Ensure they are properly charged.
- **Check Charging Port**: Make sure the charging port is clean and free of debris. A poor connection can result in insufficient charging.

3. Distorted or Unclear Audio

Problem: The audio quality is poor, or there's a lot of static, making it hard to understand the person on the other end.

Solution:

- **Adjust the Squelch**: If there's excessive background noise, adjust the squelch control. This will help reduce static and only allow clear transmissions through. Be careful not to set it too high, or you might miss faint signals.
- **Reduce Interference**: Other electronic devices or radios operating on the same frequency can cause interference. Try changing the channel to see if the issue persists.
- **Check the Microphone**: Ensure the microphone is clear of obstructions and that you're speaking directly into it. Some radios may also have a mic sensitivity setting; adjust it for better clarity.

4. Unable to Transmit (Radio is Not Sending a Signal)

Problem: When you press the **PTT (Push-to-Talk)** button, the radio does not transmit.

Solution:

- **Check the Frequency**: Ensure you are on a GMRS-approved channel. If you're using an incorrect channel or frequency, transmission won't work.
- **Check License**: GMRS radios require a license to operate legally. If you're operating without one, the radio won't transmit legally. Double-check that your license is valid and active.

- **Verify Power Settings**: If the radio is set to **low power**, you might experience transmission issues, especially over long distances. Switch to **high power** mode if needed.
- **Battery Check**: If the battery is too low, your radio may not transmit. Make sure your radio has enough charge before trying again.
- **Radio Lock**: Some radios have a **keypad lock** that prevents accidental transmission. Ensure the lock is off, and try transmitting again.

5. Radio Not Turning On

Problem: The radio won't turn on, even after pressing the power button.

Solution:

- **Check Battery**: A dead or improperly installed battery is the most common cause. Ensure the battery is properly seated and charged. If using rechargeable batteries, make sure they are correctly connected and have sufficient charge.
- **Inspect the Power Switch**: If the power switch is loose or broken, the radio may fail to turn on. Ensure the power button is functioning properly.
- **Try a Different Battery**: If the radio still doesn't turn on, the battery might be defective. Try replacing the battery with a fully charged one.

6. Radio Overheating

Problem: The radio becomes hot during use or charging.

Solution:

- **Avoid Extended Use on High Power**: Continuous use on high power settings can cause the radio to overheat. If the radio is becoming hot, switch to lower power or take breaks during use.
- **Check Charging Setup**: If the radio gets too hot while charging, disconnect it and let it cool down before attempting to charge it again. Check the charging cable and ensure it's functioning properly.
- **Ensure Proper Ventilation**: Keep the radio in a well-ventilated area while using or charging it. Avoid covering the radio with items that could block airflow.

7. Unable to Connect to a Repeater

Problem: You're unable to connect to a repeater, even though the settings seem correct.

Solution:

- **Check Repeater Settings**: Verify that the radio is set to the correct repeater frequency and shift (positive or negative). Repeaters require specific frequencies for both transmission and reception.
- **Verify Repeater Availability**: Ensure the repeater you're trying to access is actually functioning and within range. Some repeaters may be down for maintenance or unavailable due to technical issues.
- **Antenna Position**: If you're not getting a strong signal from the repeater, try adjusting the antenna to improve reception. Elevating the antenna or moving to a higher location can improve the connection.

8. Channel Interference

Problem: There's too much interference or cross-talk on the selected channel.

Solution:

- **Switch Channels**: If there's too much interference, try switching to a different GMRS channel. Some channels may be more crowded than others, especially in populated areas.
- **Use Privacy Codes (CTCSS/DCS)**: Applying a **privacy code** (CTCSS or DCS) will help filter out transmissions from other users on the same channel, reducing interference and ensuring that you can hear only relevant communication.
- **Check for Nearby Electronics**: Other electronics, such as nearby radios, microwaves, or Wi-Fi routers, may interfere with GMRS signals. Try to distance yourself from such equipment to reduce interference.

9. No Sound from the Speaker

Problem: There's no sound coming from the speaker, even though the radio is turned on.

Solution:

- **Check the Volume**: Ensure that the **volume control** is turned up. Sometimes, the volume might accidentally be set to low or muted.
- **Check for External Devices**: If you're using an external speaker or headset, ensure it's properly connected. Sometimes the radio may be outputting sound to an external device instead of the built-in speaker.
- **Inspect the Speaker**: If you're still getting no sound, the internal speaker might be damaged. Check the radio for any visible signs of damage or distortion. If necessary, consult the manufacturer for repairs.

10. Intermittent Transmissions or Dropouts

Problem: Your transmission cuts in and out or drops unexpectedly.

Solution:

- **Check Battery Power**: Low battery power can cause intermittent transmission. Ensure the battery is charged and properly connected.
- **Move to a Better Location**: If you're in an area with lots of obstacles, such as hills or buildings, your signal may drop due to poor reception. Try moving to a more open location for better signal quality.
- **Inspect the Antenna**: A loose or damaged antenna can cause the signal to drop in and out. Ensure the antenna is securely attached and in good condition.

Maintaining Your GMRS Radio for Longevity

The battery is one of the first things to remember. Taking care of the battery is important because it is what makes your GMRS radio work. Always use replaceable batteries of the right quality for your radio model. If you regularly let the battery run all the way, it can lose some of its power over time. Also, make sure the radio is charged right. The battery's life can be cut short by overcharging or undercharging it. If you're not going to be using the radio for a while, take out the battery and store it somewhere else. That way, it won't drain or damage the device.

The antenna is the next important part that needs to be taken care of regularly. To make sure it works well, the antenna should be kept clean and free of damage. Check it often for cracks, breaks, or bends that show it's been used. If the antenna can be taken off, make sure it is securely attached so it doesn't come loose or get broken while you're using it. If you see any problems with the antenna, you might want to get a new one to keep the radio's signal strong.

A lot of people don't pay much attention to the radio's case, but it does cover the internal parts. Keep dust, dirt, and water away from the radio. If you use it in a rough place, wipe it down with a soft cloth every time to get rid of any dirt or dust that could damage it over time. If heavy dirt or wetness gets on your radio, you might want to use a protected case to keep it from getting damaged. Also, store the radio somewhere safe when not in use so that it doesn't get dropped or hit something hard, which could damage the case or the parts inside.

The buttons and links are another important part to pay attention to. These are places that can break down or stop responding as well if they are not taken care of properly. A soft, dry cloth should be used every so often to clean the buttons, knobs, and microphone port.

Don't use mics or speakers when they're not being used. This will keep the connections from wearing out. If the knobs or buttons feel sticky or don't work, you might want to clean them gently or get them repaired to make sure they keep working.

Check the charging port often on radios that have docks or cords for charging from the outside. Dirt or rust in the charging port can make it impossible for the radio to charge properly. To clean the charging port, use a dry cloth or compressed air. Also, make sure the wire connects securely. If charging doesn't work right, like charging slowly or not at all, check the cord for wear and replace it if it's worn out.

Lastly, make sure that your GMRS radio's software and settings are always up to date. Some radios let you change the software to make them work better or add new features. If you check for these updates on a regular basis and load them, your radio will keep working well and be able to handle any changes in technology or rules.

How to Maximize Battery Life

1. Turn Off Unnecessary Features

Voice-activated communication (VOX), lights, and dual watch are just a few of the extra features that many GMRS radios have that can quickly drain the battery. These functions are useful sometimes, but they should be turned off when they're not being used. As an example, VOX starts communication immediately when sound is recognized, and the backlight uses extra power. Turning these features off when they're not needed can save a lot of battery life.

2. Lower the Volume

When the volume is turned up, the radio needs more power. If you don't need the sound to be at its highest level, turn it down. This helps a lot when you're somewhere quiet or when someone is talking on the radio close by. Keeping the noise at the right level will keep the battery from dying faster than it needs to.

3. Use Power-Saving Mode

Some GMRS radios have a mode or setting called "low power" that saves power. This function helps you use less power when you're not sending or in standby mode. In the power-saving mode, the radio can last longer on a single charge when it's not being used for conversation. However, it will fail when you need to transmit.

4. Use High Power Sparingly

A lot of GMRS radios have a switch that lets you choose between high-power and low-power delivery. The signal is stronger over longer distances when the power is high, but the battery dies faster. Only use high power when you have to, like when you need to talk to someone far away or in a place with a lot of interruption. To save battery life, use the low power setting for everyday conversation.

5. Avoid Frequent Transmissions

The radio uses power to transmit whenever you press the Push-to-Talk (PTT) button. While transmitting, the battery will die faster the more you do it. Cut down on transfer time to save power. Try to make your texts short and to the point, and don't send anything that isn't important.

6. Turn Off When Not in Use

To keep the battery from dying needlessly, turn off your GMRS radio when you're not using it. This is especially important when you don't do anything for a long time, like when you're sleeping or waiting for someone to call you. Just remember to turn off your radio when you're not using it. This will save battery life and keep it ready for when you need it.

7. Monitor Battery Levels Regularly

Listen to your radio and pay attention to the battery light. You can see how much power is left on many GMRS radios by looking at the screen. If you don't want to run out of power without warning, charge the battery as soon as it starts to run low. Checking the battery often helps make sure you always have enough power for important calls.

8. Use a High-Quality Rechargeable Battery

The battery in your radio has a big effect on how long it lasts and how well it works. Always use a portable battery made for GMRS radios that is of good quality. Most of the time, these batteries work better and last longer than cheaper ones. Buy lithium-ion batteries if you can. They are known for being efficient and lasting a long time.

9. Keep the Battery Contacts Clean

When battery contacts are dirty or rusted, they can't move power as well, which means the battery drains faster. Both the battery and the radio's contacts should be cleaned often to make sure they work well together. Remove any dust, dirt, or rust with a dry cloth or a soft brush. Keeping the battery contacts in good shape helps power flow and extends the life of the battery.

10. Store Batteries Properly

Don't use your GMRS radio for a while, then take out the battery and store it somewhere else. Leaving a battery in the radio for a long time can make it drain faster and hurt its health in general. Keep your batteries in a cool, dry place. Don't leave them in full sunlight or places that are too hot, as these can also cause the batteries to wear out faster.

CHAPTER 10

GMRS RADIO ACCESSORIES

Essential Accessories for GMRS Radios

1. Antenna Upgrades

One of the most important things that determines the range and accuracy of transmission on GMRS radios is how well the antenna works. Even though most radios come with a basic antenna, switching to a better or longer-range antenna can make it much easier to send and receive signals.

- **External Antennas**: There are also external antennas, which are great for travel radios and base station setups. When compared to stock antennas, external antennas usually have stronger signals and cover more ground.
- **Magnetic Mount Antennas**: These antennas are great for use on the go or in a car. When you're on the go, you can talk to people better because you can connect them to the roof of your car or any metal surface.
- **Dual-Band Antennas**: These are great for people who need both GMRS and other frequencies, like VHF/16 GHz.

2. Battery Packs and Power Solutions

GMRS radios can have different battery lives based on how they are used and what kind of cells are used. Having reliable and long-lasting power options is important to make sure you never lose contact in important situations.

- **Rechargeable Batteries**: Many GMRS radios are compatible with rechargeable battery packs, such as NiMH (Nickel-Metal Hydride) or Li-ion (Lithium-Ion) batteries. These are not only cost-effective in the long run but also eco-friendly since they can be reused multiple times.
- **Spare Battery Packs**: Carrying extra battery packs is a smart choice for extended trips or in situations where you can't easily recharge. Having backup batteries ensures you stay connected for longer periods.

- **Battery Charging Stations**: If you have multiple GMRS radios or spare batteries, a charging station can be a convenient way to keep them all powered up. Some charging stations are designed to charge several batteries simultaneously, which can be a time-saver.
- **Vehicle Adapters**: For those who use GMRS radios in their cars or on off-road adventures, a vehicle adapter can allow you to charge your radio directly from the car's power outlet, keeping your communication lines open even during long trips.

3. Headsets and Earpieces

Headsets and earpieces are necessary tools for GMRS radios so that you can talk more clearly and use the radio without using your hands. With these add-ons, you can get better sound quality, especially in busy places, and talk to people while keeping your hands free.

- **Single and Dual Earpiece Headsets**: These are helpful when you need to listen to the radio without bothering other people. Most of the time, they have mics built in, which makes them a good choice for use on the go.
- **Boom Microphones**: Boom mics send high-quality voice signals and are often used in business settings where clear contact is very important. With these add-ons, you can use the radio without using your hands, and your words will still be picked up perfectly.
- **Push-to-Talk (PTT) Adapters**: Some headsets have a PTT button, which is an important function that lets you transmit messages without touching the radio. This is very useful when you're doing things like riding a bike, camping, or driving.

4. Carrying Cases and Holsters

Buying holsters or carrying cases for your GMRS radio is a good idea if you want to keep it safe and easy to get to. These add-ons help keep your radio safe from damage and make it less likely that you'll lose it in the field.

- **Soft Cases and Pouches**: These cases protect your phone from scratches, dirt, and small drops. They also make it easy to attach your GMRS radio to your belt or backpack so you can get to it quickly.

- **Hard Cases**: A hard case is the best way to protect your phone from drops and rough surroundings. Most of the time, these cases are waterproof and shockproof, so your GMRS radio will still work even when things get rough.
- **Wearable Holsters**: Some holsters are made to be worn on the chest, waist, or shoulder. This makes them easy to get to and frees up your hands for other jobs. These holsters are great for work in the field, shooting, and other outdoor activities.

5. Microphones and Speakers

Adding external mics and speakers can really help with sound quality and comfort, especially in places with a lot of background noise or when using the GMRS radio for work or emergencies.

- **External Microphones**: When there is a lot of background noise, external mics often pick up sound better than the radio's built-in microphones. Some models have noise-canceling features that help block out background noise so that messages are clearer.
- **External Speakers**: If you're in a noisy place or need to hear your conversation better, external speakers can make the sound louder and clearer than the built-in speaker. Plus, you can use these speakers with outside mics to boost the sound of both sending and receiving.
- **Portable Speaker-Microphone Combos**: These are small devices that combine the microphone and speaker functions into one unit. They make contact easier and more convenient all in one package.

6. GMRS Radio Holder Kits

The radio fixing kit is necessary to keep the device in place and make it easy to use while moving for mobile radios that are used in cars. Mounting kits make sure that your GMRS radio is set up so that it is easy to get to and doesn't get in the way of your view or the settings for your car.

- **Dashboard and Console Mounts**: These mounts let you put your GMRS radio on the dashboard or console of your car, where it will be stable and easy to reach.
- **Suction Cup Mounts**: Another way to briefly protect your GMRS radio is to use a suction cup fix on the windshield or another smooth surface.

You can easily take them off, which makes them great for rental cars or short-term setups.

7. GMRS Repeaters

If you want to get a better range and service, a GMRS repeater can be very useful, especially if you're using a cell or base station radio. Retransmitting radio messages to make the range between radios longer so that people can talk over longer distances is what a GMRS repeater does.

- **Repeater Stations**: An antenna, an emitter, and a receiver make up a repeater station. The repeater station picks up and repeats the signal when you transmit it on a GMRS frequency, boosting its power and range.
- **Portable Repeaters**: These are smaller, easier-to-carry repeater stations that can be used in the field or for short-term setups. They are often used in places that are hard to reach by car or where radio signals don't work well.

8. GMRS Radio Software and Programming Cables

Software and programming cords can be very important for people who want to change the settings or frequencies on their GMRS radios. With these add-ons, users can program particular channels, change the power settings, or set up their own frequencies to suit their needs.

- **Programming Cables**: These are USB cables that connect your GMRS radio to a computer. Through compatible software, you can upload and download channel settings, frequency data, and other preferences to the radio.
- **Software Programs**: Many GMRS radios come with specific software that enables users to easily program their devices. These programs often provide a more detailed and precise method for setting up radios, making them ideal for people who need to fine-tune their equipment for specific use cases.

How to Choose the Right Antenna

1. Understand Your GMRS Radio's Antenna Options

There may be more than one way to improve the antenna that comes with most GMRS radios, but it depends on the type. Before you choose an antenna, you should know what kind of radio you have (handheld, mobile, or base station) and what kinds of connections it has. When it comes to GMRS radios, the two main types of antennas are

- **Whip Antennas**: These are the antennas that are most often used with small GMRS radios. They're bendable and usually connect right to the radio. If you can talk to someone in clear sight, they work well, but their range may not be as long as other types of antennas.
- **External Antennas**: When it comes to mobile radios or base stations, external antennas are often used. These antennas can be placed outside of a car or home. They have a longer range and a stronger signal, which is useful in places with barriers or when talking over long distances.

2. Consider the Frequency Range

GMRS radios can only work in a certain frequency band, which is usually between 462.550 MHz and 467.725 MHz. Make sure that the radio you choose works with this frequency range. Some antennas are made to work on certain frequency bands, like VHF and UHF. Other antennas, called wideband antennas, can cover a wider range of frequencies, such as GMRS.

- **Dual-Band Antennas**: If you use your GMRS radio for other services, like amateur radio or the VHF/UHF bands, you might want to get an antenna that works with both bands. For multi-frequency transmission, these antennas are useful because they can transmit and receive signals on both VHF and UHF frequencies.

3. Look at the Gain

Antenna gain is a measure of how well an antenna turns electrical power into radio waves that travel in a certain direction. A wider range is generally a sign of higher gain, but it can also change the pattern of radiation and receiving.

- **Low Gain Antennas (2–5 dB):** These antennas transmit and receive messages in all directions equally well. They work great for short-range contact and are perfect for hand-held radios or talking to people in the same area.
- **High Gain Antennas (6–12 dB):** These antennas focus the signal in one direction, which lets you talk to people farther away. They work great with mobile radios and base stations that need to talk to people far away. Remember that an antenna with a higher gain might cut down on the vertical waves, which could make it less effective in some areas.

4. Consider the Antenna Type and Mounting Style

The range and ease of use will depend on the type of antenna you use and how it is mounted (handheld, mobile, or base).

- **Magnetic Mount Antennas**: These antennas are magnetic and can be quickly attached to any metal surface. They are great for mobile GMRS sets in cars, trucks, or RVs. They have a long-range and are small and light, so you can use them anywhere.
- **External Vehicle Antennas**: If you're using a cell phone radio, you can choose an external antenna that is placed on the roof or the hood. These kinds of antennas are usually put in place permanently and are better at picking up signals than internal ones.
- **Base Station Antennas**: To make your home or office base station's range longer, you should get an outdoor high-gain antenna that you can put on a roof, tower, or pole. Long-distance contact is made possible by base station antennas, which can be made to handle high power outputs (up to 50 watts) on GMRS frequencies.

5. Check the Build Quality and Durability

If you want to use your antenna in rough, outdoor places, it's especially important that it lasts a long time. A well-built antenna will last a long time and work reliably.

- **Material**: Most antennas are made of metal, plastic, or stainless steel. Stainless steel is strong and flexible at the same time, and fiberglass lasts a long time and doesn't rust. Aluminum antennas are light, but they might not be as flexible.
- **Weather Resistance**: If you're going to use the antenna outside, you should pick one that can handle a range of weather conditions. Look for antennas that have coats that are resistant to weather or UV light. This is especially important for mobile or base station antennas that will be outside.

6. Consider the Mounting Location and Space Constraints

What kind and how big of an antenna you should use will depend on where you plan to put it.

- **Handheld Radio**: If you're using a handheld GMRS radio, you won't have many options for how to place the antenna, so you'll have to use the base or improved whip antenna that comes with the radio.
- **Vehicle or Mobile Setup**: If you want to place the antenna on a car, think about the height, shape, and number of fixing areas that are available. Permanent mounts last longer and are more stable, while magnetic mounts are easy to put on and take off.
- **Base Station Setup**: For base stations, make sure you have enough room to place the receiver. The best performance will come from an antenna that is placed on a roof or a pole, but you'll need to think about the room you have and any local rules that might apply to installing an antenna.

7. Regulatory Considerations

Before you put up an antenna, make sure you know what the local zoning laws or rules are about where they can go. There may be rules about the height or placement of antennas in some places, especially if you are putting one in your home or a car.

- **FCC Compliance**: GMRS radios are regulated by the Federal Communications Commission (FCC) in the United States. Ensure that any antenna you choose complies with FCC regulations, especially if you're planning to use a high-power antenna with mobile or base station radios.

8. Budget and Value

It's important to choose the antenna that gives you the best value for your money, even though high-performance antennas tend to cost more. Think about how much the antenna costs compared to how much better it will work.

- **Entry-Level Antennas**: If you are new to GMRS and just need an antenna to get started, an entry-level antenna with moderate gain and durability should suffice. You can always upgrade later as your needs evolve.
- **High-End Antennas**: For those seeking maximum range and performance, high-gain antennas, though more expensive, are ideal for professional users or those who require long-distance communication.

9. Installation and Ease of Use

When choosing an antenna, think about how simple it is to set up. Some antennas come with full installation kits that include all the fastening tools and instructions you need, while others may need extra parts that you have to buy separately.

- **Plug-and-Play Antennas**: These antennas are typically easy to install and require minimal tools. They are great for beginners or users who want to avoid complicated setups.
- **Advanced Antennas**: These might require more technical expertise for installation, such as professional antenna tuning or custom mountings. However, they typically offer superior performance and range.

When picking the right antenna for your GMRS radio, you need to think about things like the type of antenna, frequency compatibility, strength, sturdiness, and how it needs to be installed. Choosing the right antenna can make your communication experience much better, whether you need it for car use, mobile contact, or setting up a base station. Always pick an antenna that works well with your needs and the area you're in, and don't be afraid to spend more on a better antenna if you need more range or solid performance.

Upgrading Your GMRS Radio for Better Performance

Upgrading your GMRS radio can make it work much better, giving you greater contact, a longer range, and more reliable service. You can make your GMRS radio better by upgrading it the right way, whether you're using it for fun, work, or an emergency. This is a complete guide on how to improve the performance of your GMRS radio.

1. Upgrade the Antenna

The antenna is one of the most important parts of your GMRS radio. You can improve both your receiving and sending range by getting a better antenna. Most stock antennas don't have a lot of range, so adding an extra antenna with more power can make your radio much more useful.

Change to a longer whip antenna if you're using a small GMRS radio. It can make the signal stronger. An outside antenna is best for travel radios. Permanent mounts, like roof or fender-mounted antennas, are better for long-term use and stability. Magnetic mount antennas are great for short-term setups. Furthermore, dual-band radios give you more options if you need to talk on multiple frequencies, and they work better if you also use VHF or UHF bands.

2. Improve Battery Life and Power Supply

Many GMRS radios run on batteries, so making sure your radio has a stable and long-lasting power source is important for regular contact. Many GMRS radios come with batteries that can be charged, but if you buy a high-capacity battery pack, you can go longer without charging it.

You might want to buy extra battery packs so you're never without power, especially on long trips or in case of an emergency. It's also easy to keep track of power for multiple radios or extra batteries with charging units that can charge multiple batteries at once. For those who use radios in cars, adapters that let you charge straight from the power port in your car can be lifesavers on long trips or off-road excursions.

3. Add a Speaker and Microphone for Better Audio Quality

Good audio clarity is important for communicating, especially when you're far away or in a noisy place. Most GMRS radios have speakers and mics built in, but microphones and speakers that are connected to the radio from the outside can provide much better sound quality.

Adding a boom microphone or headset to your radio, for instance, can enhance your ability to transmit clear messages even in windy or busy areas. These add-ons can help your words be picked up better and block out unwanted noise. In the same way, an external speaker with a higher volume can help you hear new texts better in noisy places, which makes it easier to talk to people.

4. For Longer Range, Use a Repeater

A GMRS repeater can help you increase the range of your radio if you need to talk over long distances, especially in places with weak signal coverage. You can speak over a much longer distance than the radio alone could by using repeaters, which work as relay stations to receive and transmit your signal.

Adding a repeater to your base station or car setup can give you a lot more service in rural areas or when you're going through mountains or valleys where you can't talk directly to your base station. There are also portable repeaters for people who need a quick fix in remote places.

5. Optimize the Mounting Setup for Mobile Radios

If you're using a mobile GMRS radio in your car, making sure the radio is mounted correctly can greatly improve its range and usefulness. When the radio and its antenna are set up correctly, they are placed so that they receive and send signals as efficiently as possible.

Buying good mounts for your radio will keep it firmly in place while you travel, stopping any vibrations or changes that could make it hard to talk. Antennas that are placed on the roof or the fender are best for clear communication with no interference. These setups will make sure that your mobile GMRS radio works well even when you're moving.

6. Software and Programming Upgrades

With the right software and programming cables, you can change and program some GMRS radios to work with certain frequencies, channels, or power settings. This is especially true for more complicated models. You can fine-tune the settings on your radio to suit your needs by updating the software. For example, you can change the power output or add your own stations.

Setting up your radio and computer can be easy with programming cords. This gives you full control over your device. If your GMRS radio lets you, you can set up special channels for things like family talk, emergency functions, or group activities.

7. Add a Protective Case

It is very important that your GMRS radio is durable, especially if you plan to use it in rough terrain. Some radios come with basic cases to protect them, but buying a good, tough case can keep your radio from getting broken by drops, dirt, or water. A waterproof case will keep your radio working perfectly even when things get rough.

Cases that are waterproof and shockproof are available for people who want to use their radios in harsh outdoor situations, like when they are hiking, off-roading, or swimming. Your radio will stay working when you need it most thanks to these bags that protect it from both physical damage and the weather.

8. Upgrade to a Higher-Powered Radio

If your current GMRS radio doesn't give you enough range or service, you might want to consider getting a more powerful one. Upgrading to a model with a higher wattage will greatly improve your range because GMRS radios can transmit up to 50 watts of power.

For instance, if you're using a small GMRS radio that can only put out 5 watts of power, you might want to switch to a mobile or base station radio that can put out more power. When used with the right antenna setup, these radios usually have better range and performance.

CHAPTER 11

UNDERSTANDING GMRS REGULATIONS AND LAWS

Legal Usage of GMRS Radios

General Mobile Radio Service (GMRS) radios are a useful way to talk to people in both personal and business situations. However, like many other radio services, they are regulated by the law. These rules make sure that the GMRS radio frequencies are used properly so that they don't interfere with other phone systems. It is important to know and follow the laws when using GMRS to avoid fines and make sure communication is safe and effective. Here is an in-depth look at how GMRS radios can be legally used:

1. Licensing Requirement

Getting a license from the Federal Communications Commission (FCC) is one of the most important necessary steps for using GMRS radios in the United States. Unlike some other radio services, like FRS or CB, you need a license to properly use GMRS.

- **Who Needs a License**: A GMRS license is required by anyone who operates a GMRS radio, whether it's for personal or family use. The license is typically issued to an individual, and the license covers the individual's immediate family members, including spouses and children.
- **How to Obtain a License**: To obtain a GMRS license, you must apply through the FCC. The application process can be completed online via the FCC's Universal Licensing System (ULS). There is a fee for applying, and the license is generally valid for 10 years.
- **License Renewal**: After 10 years, the GMRS license must be renewed. However, the FCC no longer requires an examination or test for GMRS licenses, making the process straightforward. The renewal fee is typically lower than the original application fee.

2. Operating Frequency and Power Limits

In the 462 MHz and 467 MHz bands, GMRS works on certain frequencies. Some services, like FRS (Family Radio Service), use the same frequencies. GMRS, on the other hand, can send data with more power, which makes its range longer.

- **Allocating Frequencies**: The FCC sets the GMRS frequencies, which can't be used for anything else without permission. GMRS frequencies that are often used are 462.550 MHz, 462.575 MHz, 462.600 MHz, and others in the same band.
- **Power Requirements**: GMRS radios can transmit at higher power levels than FRS radios, but mobile radios can only transmit at a maximum of 50 watts. Most handheld GMRS radios can only handle 5 watts of power. The power cap makes sure that using a GMRS radio doesn't get in the way of other types of contact, like emergency and business calls.

3. Limitations on Use

GMRS radios are limited in a number of important ways to keep them from being abused or interfering with other stations.

- **Non-Business Use**: GMRS radios are meant to be used for talking to family and friends. It is illegal to use GMRS radios for business reasons, like running a business. Businesses must use other radio services that are approved for commercial use instead of GMRS because it is only for private use.
- **Don't Broadcast:** GMRS radios aren't meant to be used for streaming. Users are not allowed to send or transmit unsolicited texts. Messages should only be used for private conversations, like those with family or friends.
- **No Communications with Third Parties**: GMRS users can't use the radios to send texts to people who aren't in their close family or home. This limit stops people from communicating or using the service in a way that isn't allowed.
- **Interference with Other Services**: People who use GMRS radios must make sure that their radios don't conflict with other radio services in a way that is damaging. This means keeping an eye on

nearby services, like emergency contact networks, to make sure that GMRS broadcasts don't get in the way of important work.

4. Use of Repeaters

By getting a signal and sending it again on a different frequency, repeaters help GMRS radios communicate over longer distances. People often use repeaters to make sure they can talk clearly over longer distances, especially in places with physical barriers like mountains.

- **Using Repeaters and Getting a License**: It is allowed to use GMRS repeaters, but the person running the repeater needs to get a license from the FCC. Repeater can be used to improve coverage by approved GMRS users, but they must follow the rules set by the FCC.
- **Coordination and Compliance**: Repeater users may need to work with local repeater networks or groups to make sure their repeaters don't interact with other repeaters. This teamwork helps make sure that all GMRS users can communicate clearly and quickly.

5. Rules for Mobile and Base Station Use

GMRS radios can be used in mobile (on a car) or base station (fixed) setups, but there are legal rules about how they can be used.

- **Vehicle Mounting**: Mobile GMRS radios can be properly used in cars as long as the person operating them has a current GMRS license. The FCC rules say that these radios must be set up and used in a certain way, including following the power limits.
- **Base Stations**: These are usually more powerful radios that are used in homes or businesses. They are also limited in power and license. These base stations are great for people who need a longer range or who need to work in rural places.

6. Cross-Band Service and Other Options

GMRS radios are made to work with GMRS frequencies. Based on the type, though, some GMRS radios may also be able to work on other frequencies, like FRS or even amateur radio bands. So, here are some law things to think about.

- **Cross-Band Operation**: It is legal to use a radio to talk on more than one band, like the GMRS and amateur radio bands, but the person doing so must follow the licensing rules for each band. For example, you don't need an amateur radio license to use GMRS, but you do need one to use amateur frequencies. You can get an amateur radio license from the FCC.
- **Interference with Other Services**: It is illegal and can lead to fines to use GMRS radios on frequencies outside of the allowed GMRS range without the right licenses. People who use GMRS must make sure they stay within the frequencies and power limits that are set for GMRS transmission.

7. International Usage

There are rules about how to use GMRS radios in the US, but it can be harder to follow those rules when traveling abroad. Radio frequency rules vary from country to country, and using GMRS radios outside of the U.S. may be against the law there.

- **Licensing in Other Countries**: If you want to use GMRS radios in another country, you should check with that country's telecommunications body to see if it is legal to do so. Different countries often have different rules or may need their own licenses to use radio.
- **Frequency Compatibility**: GMRS frequencies may not be the same in other countries, so using a GMRS radio made in the U.S. could mess up contact systems in other countries. It is very important to make sure that any radio gear you use follows the rules and frequencies in your area.

8. Penalties for Non-Compliance

People can get in trouble if they don't follow the rules about GMRS radios. These rules are enforced by the FCC. People who break them may get fines, other punishments, or their GMRS license taken away. Here are some common violations:

- Operating without a valid license.
- Interfering with other communication services.

- Using GMRS radios for commercial purposes.
- Operating at unauthorized power levels or frequencies.

To properly use GMRS radios, you need to get a license from the FCC, follow power limits and frequency assignments, and follow other rules about how to use the radios. These laws make sure that GMRS contact stays quick, and clear, and doesn't get in the way of other important communication services. People who use GMRS can communicate clearly over long distances without getting in trouble with the law as long as they know and follow the rules.

Tips for Staying Compliant with GMRS Regulations

Following the rules for GMRS (General Mobile Radio Service) is important to make sure that your connection stays legal, works well, and doesn't mess with other services. There are rules that must be followed, and if you don't, the Federal Communications Commission (FCC) can fine you or take away your GMRS license. Here are some useful tips to help you follow the rules set by GMRS:

Obtain and Maintain a Valid GMRS License

One of the most critical aspects of GMRS compliance is holding a valid GMRS license issued by the FCC. Without it, you are not legally allowed to operate GMRS radios. Here's how to stay compliant:

- **Apply for a License**: Make sure to apply for a GMRS license through the FCC's Universal Licensing System (ULS). The process is simple, and the license covers your entire immediate family (spouse, children, etc.).
- **Renew on Time**: Your GMRS license is valid for 10 years. Set a reminder to renew it before it expires to avoid any lapses in your ability to legally operate your radios.
- **Family Coverage**: The license extends to your immediate family members, so ensure that everyone who will be using GMRS radios is covered by your license.

Follow the Power Limitations

GMRS radios are allowed higher power output than other radio services like FRS (Family Radio Service). However, there are strict limits on how much power you can use:

- **Handheld Radios**: The power output for handheld GMRS radios is limited to 5 watts. Be mindful of this when using portable devices.
- **Mobile Radios**: If you use a mobile GMRS radio in your vehicle, the power output can be as high as 50 watts. Make sure to stay within this limit to avoid violating FCC regulations.
- **Monitor Power Settings**: Regularly check your radio's power settings to ensure you're not exceeding the legal limit. Some radios have settings that allow you to adjust the power output, so make sure you're using the appropriate setting for your needs.

Use Only Authorized GMRS Frequencies

GMRS radios are authorized to operate on specific frequencies within the 462 MHz and 467 MHz bands. Ensure that you're only transmitting on these designated channels:

- **Stick to GMRS Channels**: Familiarize yourself with the GMRS frequencies, such as 462.550 MHz, 462.575 MHz, and others within the 462 MHz and 467 MHz ranges. Don't use frequencies that are not allocated for GMRS use, as doing so can cause interference with other services.
- **Avoid FRS Frequencies**: GMRS and FRS share some frequencies, but GMRS radios are allowed to transmit at higher power levels on those frequencies. Ensure that you're only using the designated GMRS frequencies and not exceeding power limits on shared channels.

Avoid Commercial Use

GMRS radios are strictly for personal and family use. They are not authorized for commercial or business purposes. To stay compliant:

- **Use for Personal Communication Only**: GMRS radios should be used for personal, non-commercial communication with family, friends, or groups. Using GMRS radios for business operations or to relay business-related messages is prohibited.

- **Separate Business and Personal Use**: If you need radios for business purposes, consider using a different service (like the business bands of FRS, MURS, or commercial radio services), as GMRS is only licensed for personal use.

Respect Other Radio Services

To avoid interfering with other services, it's essential to operate your GMRS radio responsibly. Keep the following in mind:

- **Avoid Interference**: GMRS communications should not cause interference with emergency services, commercial radio, or other licensed radio services. Always ensure you are transmitting on the correct frequencies and within the designated power limits to prevent interference.
- **Use Short Transmissions**: Long, unnecessary transmissions can cause interference, especially in crowded radio bands. Use short, clear messages, and keep your radio usage minimal to reduce the risk of interfering with others.
- **Be Mindful of Repeaters**: If you're using a GMRS repeater, ensure it is properly coordinated with local networks to avoid interference with other repeaters or radio services.

Don't Use GMRS for Broadcasting

GMRS radios are designed for private, two-way communication and should not be used for broadcasting. Broadcasting unlicensed messages, whether for entertainment, information, or advertising, is prohibited:

- **No Public Announcements**: GMRS radios should not be used to broadcast public announcements, music, or advertisements. Keep transmissions limited to personal or family communication.
- **Respect Privacy**: Avoid using GMRS to transmit unsolicited or unwanted messages. Always ensure that your communications are private and necessary.

Properly Install and Maintain Your Equipment

To ensure that your GMRS radio setup is fully compliant, take care when installing and maintaining your equipment:

- **Install Antennas Correctly**: Whether you're using a mobile radio or a base station, make sure your antenna is installed according to manufacturer recommendations. This ensures optimal performance and reduces the risk of interference with other services.
- **Use Quality Equipment**: When upgrading antennas, radios, or other accessories, ensure that the equipment is compliant with FCC regulations. Some third-party accessories may not be designed for use on GMRS frequencies, so always check for compatibility.
- **Maintain Equipment**: Regularly check and maintain your radios and antennas to ensure they're functioning properly. Faulty or poorly maintained equipment can lead to poor communication performance and increase the risk of interference.

Use GMRS Repeaters Responsibly

Repeaters are an effective way to extend the range of your GMRS communication, but they come with additional rules:

- **License for Repeaters**: If you plan to operate a GMRS repeater, ensure that you hold a GMRS license. Repeaters require a separate license if you intend to operate them as a relay station.
- **Coordination**: If you're using an existing GMRS repeater, check for any coordination requirements with the local repeater network to avoid interference. Ensure that you're following proper operating procedures for repeater use.

Be Aware of Legal Limitations for International Use

GMRS radios are regulated by the FCC in the U.S., but different countries have their own radio frequency regulations. If you plan to travel abroad with your GMRS radio:

- **Check Local Laws**: Before using your GMRS radio in another country, check the local telecommunications regulations to determine if GMRS frequencies are legal to use.
- **Comply with Local Licensing Requirements**: Some countries may require you to obtain a local license or use different frequencies altogether, so ensure that you understand the rules of the country you're visiting.

Stay Updated on FCC Regulations

GMRS regulations can change over time, so it's important to stay informed about any updates or changes to FCC rules. The FCC periodically reviews and updates communication regulations, and staying up to date will ensure that you're always compliant.

- **Monitor FCC Announcements**: Keep an eye on official FCC announcements, newsletters, or websites that provide updates regarding GMRS usage and rules.
- **Join GMRS User Groups**: Participating in GMRS user groups or forums can also be helpful for staying informed about new developments in GMRS regulations and best practices.

To follow GMRS rules, you must get and keep a legal license, stick to the frequency and power limits, and not use the radio for business. By following these rules and being aware of other services, you can make sure that your use of the GMRS radio is safe and useful. Keeping up with any changes to the rules and making sure your gear is in good shape will also help you keep using your GMRS radios without any problems.

CHAPTER 12

GMRS RADIO IN DIFFERENT ENVIRONMENTS

Using GMRS Radios for Outdoor Adventures

General Mobile Radio Service (GMRS) radios are very useful for outdoor activities because they let you stay in touch when cell phones might not work. GMRS radios are a reliable way to stay in touch with your group and make sure everyone stays safe while climbing, camping, off-roading, or doing other outdoor activities. To get the most out of your GMRS radios and make your journey more enjoyable, you need to know how to use them properly in the great outdoors.

Understanding the Benefits of GMRS Radios for Outdoor Adventures

GMRS radios are great for outdoor activities because they have a lot of benefits. One of the best things about them is that their range is longer than that of other mobile communication devices, like FRS radios or walkie-talkies. In some cases, GMRS radios can transmit up to 50 watts of power, greatly increasing their range. This is very important when you're in a remote place where cell service might not work or be available.

GMRS radios often have better sound quality over long distances, in addition to having a longer range. They're made to reduce static and distorting as much as possible, which is very important outside, where clear contact can make a difference in safety. Also, GMRS radios are made to work on frequencies that are only for personal contact. This makes it less likely that other services will interfere with them.

How to Pick the Best GMRS Radio for Outdoor Use

When choosing an outdoor GMRS radio, it's important to think about things like range, sturdiness, and battery life. GMRS radios come in many shapes and sizes, from small units to mobile radios that can be placed on cars. Handheld types are often the best choice for outdoor activities because they are easy to carry and use. A mobile radio with an external antenna might be better for a longer range if you plan to stay in one place or set up a base station.

Durability is another important thing to think about. Conditions outside can be rough, with dust, rain, and big changes in temperature. To make sure they work even in bad weather, look for radios that are labeled as weather-resistant or waterproof. Some types are made to military-grade standards so they can handle drops, hits, and water, which makes them perfect for off-road and outdoor trips.

For those who are going into the woods, battery life is very important. Make sure the GMRS radio you pick has a long battery life, especially if you're going on a long trip. Some radios have power packs that can be charged, while others use regular AA or lithium-ion batteries. You should bring extra batteries or a small power bank with you so you don't run out of power on your trip.

Setting Up GMRS Radios for Outdoor Communication

You need to set up your GMRS radio for your outdoor journey once you've chosen the right one for your needs. Setting up a device correctly is more than just setting it on; it's about making it work as well as possible.

To begin, make sure that your GMRS radio is set up correctly with the right bands for your group. Most GMRS radios already have standard GMRS channels put in, but you may want to program your own frequencies for certain situations. If you want to increase your range with GMRS repeaters, make sure that your radio is set to use the right repeater frequencies.

Repeater stations are very helpful in mountainous or highly wooded places where transmission may be hard to see.

Next, look at your GMRS radio's antenna. One of the most important parts for making sure good contact over long distances is the antenna. If the antenna on your mobile GMRS radio can be taken off, you might want to get a better one to get a better range. Mobile radios can get much better signal strength and range from an outside antenna that is fixed on your car, especially in places with a lot of obstacles.

Using GMRS Radios in Remote Areas

One main reason people bring GMRS radios on outdoor trips is to stay in touch in remote places. Cell towers and other forms of contact equipment are hard to find in the wilderness. This is why GMRS radios are so important for safety. They are especially helpful when hiking or camping in mountainous areas, dense woods, or along rough coasts where cell phone service isn't available.

Make sure that everyone in your group is on the same frequency so that you can talk to each other easily. Also, it's a good idea to agree on a normal way to talk to each other as a group, like a call sign or an easy way to tell who is talking. This can help clear up any misunderstandings and guarantee that messages are transmitted quickly when necessary.

The landscape can have a big effect on the range of GMRS radios in remote places. It's important to keep a clear line of sight whenever you can because mountains, valleys, and thick woods can block signals. If people in your group are spread out, GMRS repeaters can make contact much easier because they boost the signal.

GMRS radios can help your group stay in touch and avoid crashes when you're off-roading or driving in a car. For the strongest signal, you should use a mobile GMRS radio that is fixed in your car and has an antenna on the outside. Make sure that all of the cars in your group are on the same channel so that you can always talk to each other.

Safety and Emergency Use of GMRS Radios

One of the most important reasons to bring GMRS radios on outdoor trips is to stay safe. Accidents and emergencies can happen in rural areas, so it's important to be able to quickly get in touch with your group or call for help. With GMRS radios, you can stay in touch with other people and make sure that help can be sent in a situation.

Before you go into the woods, make sure that everyone in your group knows how to use the radios properly, including how to call for help. To help people in an emergency, many GMRS radios have NOAA weather channels that send out real-time weather reports or emergency messages. Some models also have GPS built-in, which lets you send out emergency messages or let other people in your group know where you are.

Also, before you go on your journey, you should make a plan for how to get in touch with people in case of an emergency. Talk about how often you'll need to check in with each other and what to do if someone gets lost or hurt. You can set times to check in via radio or pick out places where your group will meet up in case of an emergency in this plan.

Maintaining GMRS Radios During Your Adventure

It is very important to take good care of and maintain your GMRS radios while you are on an outdoor journey to make sure they work properly. Because it can get rough outside, it's important to keep your radios safe from water, dust, and damage. Many GMRS radios come with cases that cover them or are waterproof, but you should still be careful with your gear.

Watch how much you use the batteries because cold weather can drain them faster. To make sure you never run out of power, keep extra batteries or a small power bank on hand. If your radio can hold extra battery packs, you might want to bring an extra one for longer trips.

Also, make sure everything is working right by checking the antenna, battery, and any extra devices like mics or headsets on a regular basis. When using extra antennas, make sure they are properly attached and set up to get the strongest signal.

GMRS Radios in Emergency Situations

GMRS (General Mobile Radio Service) radios are useful for getting in touch during emergencies because they are a safe way to stay in touch when cell phones or other common ways of communicating are not available or have been hacked. GMRS radios are a lifeline that you can't do without during a natural tragedy when you get lost on an outdoor trip, or in any other emergency situation. Learning how to use GMRS radios correctly in an emergency can make all the difference in being able to get help, work with others, or stay aware when things get really bad.

Why GMRS Radios are Important in Emergencies

Keeping in touch with other people can mean the difference between life and death in an emergency. Communication networks often break down or get backed up during natural disasters like earthquakes, storms, and wildfires. When these things happen, GMRS radios can be a lifeline because they let people or groups stay in touch, share information, and plan rescue or escape efforts.

GMRS radios are different from regular cell phones because they don't depend on equipment that could be broken or interrupted during a disaster. They work on certain radio frequencies and let people talk directly to others, like family members, neighboring groups, or emergency workers. Because of this, GMRS radios are very important for making sure that contact stays open when it means the most.

Setting Up for Emergency Use

Before an accident happens, you should make sure your GMRS radio is ready to go. This means making sure you have the right gear, a good grasp of how to use the radio, and a plan for how to talk to people.

Make sure your GMRS radio is fully charged and has a backup power source so you can talk to people. Having extra batteries or a portable power bank is very important because power cuts can happen in an emergency. If you think you might be in an emergency situation for a long time, you might want to bring extra power packs with you.

After that, get to know the GMRS frequencies and channels that are usually used in an emergency. Emergency channels or NOAA (National Oceanic and Atmospheric Administration) weather channels that give real-time alerts and reports on bad weather are common on GMRS radios. To stay updated, you need to know how to get to these stations and set your radio to the right frequency.

Make sure that everyone in your group has their radios set to the same frequency or channel. Setting up a clear, easy-to-understand way to talk to each other can help keep things from getting confusing when things are stressful. As an example, you can all agree on certain words or call signs to use in an emergency. This way, everyone will know when someone is asking for help or needs help right away.

Using GMRS Radios for Communication During a Crisis

When there is an emergency, you can use GMRS radios to talk to different groups, like your family, friends, or the local emergency services. Most GMRS radios have a range of several miles, which makes them great for short- to medium-range contact. For example, you can use them to check in with family and friends nearby or work together with groups that are close by.

In an emergency, one of the best ways to use GMRS radios is to help everyone work together. GMRS radios let you stay in touch even when you're not with your group of walkers, campers, or off-roaders. For instance, if someone in the group gets lost or hurt, the radios let them call for help or let others know what's going on without using cell networks. GMRS radios are great for keeping in touch and making sure everyone is safe in remote places where GPS or cell service may not be available.

If there is a natural disaster, GMRS radios can help you make plans with family or friends for how to get out of the area. If the government issues escape or "shelter-in-place" orders, GMRS radios can be used to quickly and clearly send these directions. You can also use your GMRS radio to stay in touch with emergency services or neighborhood groups that are helping out during the disaster.

If you are using GMRS radios in a place with poor service, like a hilly area or a thick forest, a repeater can help you communicate further. The range over which you can speak is increased by using a GMRS extender, which receives your signal and transmits it on a different frequency. In cases where natural obstacles like mountains might get in the way of contact, this is especially helpful.

Staying Informed with GMRS Radios

Not only can GMRS radios be used to talk to other people, but they are also great for getting information in an emergency. A lot of GMRS radios have NOAA weather radio stations that send out official weather reports, warnings, and forecasts all the time. You can get updates on these stations about bad weather like storms, tornadoes, and floods, which can help you decide how to best help the situation.

GMRS radios can be used to listen for emergency messages or alerts from the government, as well as to get weather information. During some disasters, the public may receive important messages from the government and first rescuers using GMRS frequencies. Being able to listen to these reports lets you know about the latest events and get important orders, even when other ways of communicating aren't available.

If you know how to change stations and listen to emergency alerts, you can stay informed better during an emergency. You should get used to the settings on your GMRS radio before you need to use it in a situation. This will save you time when you actually need to use it.

Safety and Emergency Protocols for GMRS Use

It's important to follow certain safety and emergency rules when using GMRS radios in an emergency. First, make sure that your GMRS radio is working within the law. This is especially important if you're using a mobile or base station radio that might put out more power. Following the FCC's rules for power limits and frequency limits is important for making sure that GMRS radios don't mess with other important communication systems.

When it comes to communication methods, it's important to keep messages short and clear. In an emergency, time is of the essence, so texts that are short and to the point get the word across quickly. When there is a life-threatening situation, use common emergency phrases like "Mayday" or "SOS."

If you need to get in touch with someone right away, like in a medical emergency or during a natural disaster, use your GMRS radio to do it. Depending on how they are set up, many radios can send out emergency warning messages or direct calls to first responders. So that help can get to you as quickly as possible, be ready to give specific details, such as where you are and what the situation is.

The Role of GMRS Radios in Long-Term Emergencies

When there is a long-term emergency, like a power loss, a regional disaster, or a large-scale escape, GMRS radios can still be very useful for keeping in touch. GMRS radios let you stay in touch with other survivors, the government, or emergency service providers even when infrastructure breaks down and phone lines get too busy.

GMRS radios can also be very useful for getting information and keeping in touch with family and friends who are far away during these kinds of events. In emergencies, people are often separated, but GMRS radios help you stay in touch even if you can't use a phone or other standard methods of contact.

GMRS radios can be very useful for finding lost or separated people in areas that have been hit by disasters. You have a better chance of finding your group or other people who may need help if you use the radios to set up check-in times and places.

Best Practices for Using GMRS in Urban Areas

Using GMRS (General Mobile Radio Service) radios in cities has many benefits for personal contact, but it can also be difficult because of the noise from other electronics and the crowded surroundings. Following best practices can help you get the most out of your GMRS radio in cities while also making sure you stay in line with the law and communicate clearly. This is a complete guide on how to use GMRS radios correctly in cities.

1. Understand the Impact of Urban Environments on GMRS Performance

There are a lot of electrical gadgets, a lot of people, and tall buildings in cities, all of which can affect how well GMRS radios work. In cities, where radio signals can be blocked by metal surfaces and concrete buildings, signal interference is a major problem that can reduce the range of effective contact. In addition, many things in cities, like Wi-Fi routers, microwave ovens, and even other radio signals, can make GMRS channels silent or distorted.

In spite of these problems, GMRS radios can still be useful in towns, especially for talking over short to medium distances. Knowing what your radio can't do in a city and being ready for a shorter range are important parts of using it well.

2. Pick the Right Antenna for Use in an Urban Area

One of the most important parts of making a GMRS radio work well is the antenna. In cities, where things can get in the way of radio waves, improving your antenna can make a big difference in how far and clearly you can talk to people.

- **External Antennas**: If you use a mobile GMRS radio, you might want to put an external antenna on your car or home. Most of the time, these antennas send out better signals and are less likely to be blocked by buildings or other objects.

- **Longer or High-Gain Antennas**: Antennas that are longer or higher in gain can help improve your signal on handheld radios, especially in places where obstacles might block or lessen your transmission. These antennas not only increase range, but they can also help cut down on clutter in places with a lot of signals.
- **Magnetic Mount Antennas**: Magnetic mount antennas are a quick and easy way to set up mobile GMRS radios because they can be put on the roof of a car or any other metal surface. These antennas boost the signal strength, which is very helpful when you're traveling through crowded cities.

3. Be Mindful of Interference and Select Clear Frequencies

There is often a lot of electrical disturbance in cities, so it's important to carefully choose your GMRS channel to avoid problems. There are only a few frequencies that GMRS can use, and those frequencies are more likely to be crowded in towns.

- **Choosing a Channel**: GMRS radios are already set up with standard channels, but you might need to try a few different ones to find the one with the best signal. It's best not to use the same frequencies that are already being used by a lot of other people communicating, like business radios, emergency services, and even public service announcements.
- **Use of Repeaters**: GMRS repeaters are set up in many cities to make contact farther away. These repeaters send your signal again and can greatly improve its range and clarity, especially when there are real obstacles like buildings or other things in the way. If you want to use this service, make sure your radio can connect to area repeaters and set it to the right frequency.

4. Optimize Battery Life for Extended Communication

Communication can happen more often in busy cities, especially when you're working with other people or dealing with different scenarios. Because GMRS radios run on batteries, you need to make sure that your radio has enough power to last all day when it will be used a lot.

- **Portable Power:** If you use small radios, bring extra batteries or a portable power bank with you. For some types, the batteries can be charged, while for others, they use normal AA or lithium-ion batteries that are easy to replace with new ones.
- **Saving Battery Life**: Don't leave the radio on all the time to make the battery last longer. Instead, only use it when you have to or set up a method where you and others can check in every so often to cut down on constant messaging. Also, keep the radio on a lower power setting when you don't need to talk over long distances. This will help the battery last longer.

5. Set Up a Communication Plan with Your Group

If you want to use a GMRS radio effectively in cities, you need an organized communication plan. This is true whether you're working with a team, a family, or a group of friends. This plan helps make sure that everyone is on the same page and can help people act quickly when they need to.

- **Pre-Assigned Channels**: Set aside certain channels for different groups or reasons before you leave. One line could be used for calls in case of an emergency, and another could be used for general messages or check-ins. This makes things clearer and makes it easy for everyone in your group to find the right route for their message.
- **Emergency Procedures**: Make sure there are clear emergency procedures ahead of time. Make sure everyone knows how to signal for help, share important information, or send notes of trouble. Standardized ways of communicating, like using certain words or sentences, will help make conversations easier and speed up responses in important situations.

6. Respect Legal Regulations and License Requirements

The Federal Communications Commission (FCC) sets rules for how GMRS can be used in cities, just like for any other radio service. It's crucial to make sure that all operators have the right permissions before they transmit on GMRS frequencies because GMRS needs a license.

- **Obtain and Maintain Your License**: If you haven't already, apply for a GMRS license through the FCC. The license is valid for ten years and covers your immediate family members, so make sure to renew it when necessary. Operating without a valid license could result in fines or penalties.

- **Power Limitations**: GMRS radios have strict power limits, with handheld radios typically restricted to 5 watts of output and mobile radios limited to 50 watts. Be sure to adhere to these power limits, as exceeding them can cause interference with other communication systems and may violate FCC rules.

7. Use GMRS Radios for Short-Range Communication in Crowded Areas

When in a city, GMRS radios work best for short-range conversation. In ideal conditions, their range can go up to several miles. However, the thick infrastructure in cities can limit this range, so you should be realistic about what you can expect.

- **Short Distances and Line-of-Sight**: For GMRS radios to work best, they need to be able to see each other. If you want to send a signal better in a busy area where buildings get in the way, try to go to higher ground or a clear area. Use repeaters to make your range longer if you need to talk to people farther away or between buildings.
- **Local Communication**: GMRS radios can be used for short-range contact within a neighborhood or city block, which is useful when working with a small group. Clear communication helps to avoid depending on cell phones, which may have poor signal in some parts of the city, or to prevent cell networks from becoming overloaded during situations.

8. Stay Prepared for Unexpected Emergencies

Even in cities, situations like power outages, natural disasters, and unplanned events like traffic accidents or political unrest can happen. GMRS radios are very useful in these scenarios because they let people stay informed and plan their actions even when other ways don't work.

- **Weather Alerts and Information**: A lot of GMRS radios have NOAA weather channels that give you constant updates on the weather and emergency messages. In cities, where the weather can change quickly, keeping up with the news on your GMRS radio makes sure you are ready for any possible dangers.

- **Emergency Communication**: GMRS radios can be used as a backup way to talk in an urban situation if cell phone networks or landlines are busy or not working. You should be ready to use your radio for important conversations, like making plans to evacuate, reporting an emergency, or just keeping in touch with family and friends.

CONCLUSION

GMRS radios are a great way to stay in touch, whether you're in the middle of a disaster, out in the woods, or in a busy city. They let you talk to people far away, don't need cell towers, and work well in a variety of settings. If you know how to pick up, set up, and use your GMRS radio correctly, you'll be able to talk clearly when you need to.

Follow the license rules, pick the right setup for your needs, and be careful how you use the radio to avoid interference. You can use GMRS radios to stay in touch with a group, find out about the weather, or just make sure everyone is safe. These tips will help you get the most out of your GMRS radio, which will make your experience safer and easier.

www.ingramcontent.com/pod-product-compliance
Lightning Source LLC
LaVergne TN
LVHW062318060326
832902LV00013B/2287